AF483786

A devotional that invites you to *laugh again* with Jesus—transforming life's lemons into *faith that overflows!*

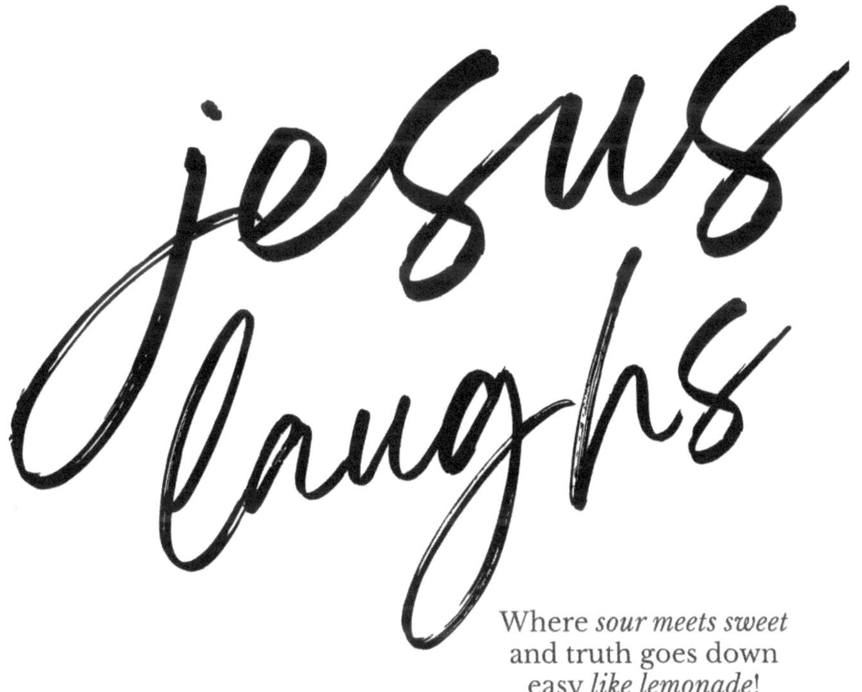

Where *sour meets sweet* and truth goes down easy *like lemonade!*

TAMRA ANDRESS

with a *collection* of authors

F.I.T. in Faith LLC
Virginia Beach, Virginia
FitInFaithPress.com
Editing: Anne Leonard
ISBN: 979-8-9928101-4-1

Dedication

This book is dedicated to the sons and daughters who long for the abundant life Jesus promised—one filled with unyielding joy. Laughing with Him is a glimpse of Heaven on earth. And that joy, intertwined with His peace, is not reserved only for sweet seasons of ease, but also for the sour moments when pain puckers every corner of our hearts. Even there, His love secures our identity and carries us into the sweetness of His presence.

Endorsements

In "Jesus Laughs," readers discover a faith that smiles, celebrates, and embraces the fullness of life. It's an inspiring and heartfelt message that reminds us joy has always been part of the Gospel.
— Cherri Bornman
Author, Speaker, Worship Leader
CherriBornman.com

"Jesus Laughs" beautifully shows us that joy isn't found in perfect circumstances, but in the redemption and beauty God brings to our most sour seasons.
— Mairin Moore Cane
Leadership Advisor | Author | Podcast Host
MairinMooreCane.com

"Jesus Laughs" reminds us that faith can include joy and humor, not just seriousness. Read it for inspiration, read it for laughs, and read it because smiling tends to create fewer wrinkles than frowning!
— Mistie Doyle
Author of "Grief is More Than Gray"

This devotional beautifully celebrates a Savior who turns our sourest sorrows into the sweetest joys, with the "lemon-to-lemonade" kind of hope that only He can provide. These stories remind me that Jesus not only weeps with us in our pain, but also celebrates with us in our delight. He is inviting every woman into a vibrant, life-giving relationship with Him.
— Amy Fast
Wife, Teen Girl Mama x3, Word Enthusiast, Holy Spirit Seeker

"Jesus Laughs" beautifully captures the truth that even in life's hardest chapters, God's delight is still present. These honest stories magnify His goodness and remind us that no moment is beyond His transforming love.
— Jen Fedorowicz
Spiritual Guide and Energy Healer
JEnergyCoach.com

This message serves as a reminder that we are nothing without Him within us. Reading it brings to mind 2 Corinthians 12:9b, where Paul states, "...For my power is made perfect in weakness." When we understand that our identity lies in who He is, we recognize that the joy of the Lord is our strength. It's not about us; it's about who He is in us and how He impacts others through us.
— Kelly Fischer
Architect of Successful Businesses, Author and Speaker
RoyalFischer.org

"Jesus Laughs" is a refreshing reminder that the gospel is good news filled with joy, redemption, and hope. Through powerful testimonies, readers are invited to rediscover the abundant Zoe life Jesus offers even in life's hardest seasons.
— April Foster
Bestselling Coauthor of "Before She Knew Jesus"
LoveColoredTheWay.com

Through Scripture, testimony, and Spirit-led wisdom, this book gently guides readers back to the heart of the Father. It reveals how God can transform even the hardest moments into something sweet when we trust His plans and remain rooted in His truth. A refreshing and hope-filled invitation to step into the fullness of life Jesus promised.
— Morgan Hart
Wife, Mother, Pastor, and Worship Leader
WordAndWorshipCo.com

God's formula for strength is JOY!!! The best way we can survive life's continuous dilemmas is through laughter. Enjoy the pages of this devotional and allow laughter to strengthen your soul.
— Reverend Kathy Holderman
IN A/G Women's, Director, Staff Pastor, Lighthouse Assembly of God, Richmond, IN

What a heartfelt devotion that demonstrates how our faith and trust in Jesus arises when we realize that the joy of the Lord is our strength during both the good and bad times. As it is written in Proverbs 17:22 (KJV), "A merry heart doeth good like a medicine."
— Linda L House
Retired Executive Registered Nurse
lindahouse1954@gmail.com

Laughter truly is a God idea, as it lightens our hearts and refreshes our souls, helping us to keep all things in proper perspective. Let these stories in "Jesus Laughs," inspire you to see more clearly the One who delights most in our enjoyment as with live free, laughing with Him.
— Jenny Ingels
Daughter of the King, PourItOutForGood.org
RestorationPoint.us

This devotional reminds us that when we align our perspective with God's truth, we can see His goodness even in life's sour seasons. I love the encouragement and renewed hope this message will bring to the hearts of those who read it.
— Amber Kennedy
Cofounder of Lose the Luggage31

This book invites you into the real-life experiences of people who have faced heartache and found redemption in Jesus alone. Every journey is different, and I trust this book will leave you deeply encouraged.
— Ruth Laskowski, M.Ed.
Founder of PROFITS Consulting

"Jesus Laughs" is a radiant reminder that our Savior doesn't waste our suffering—He transforms it. In every hard season, His joy becomes our strength, and our testimonies become living proof that redemption always has the final word.
— Barbara Mackubin
Faith-led Wellness Leader
PourItOutForGood.org

"Jesus Laughs" points readers back to the heart of God with tenderness and joy. It's a faith-building invitation to trust that even life's lemons can become holy places of surrender, healing, and delight in Christ.
— Heather O'Brien
Speaker and Prophetic Healing Coach
HeatherOBrien.net

"Jesus Laughs" is a warm hug and a beautiful reminder of the promises, character, and love of God for each of us. This devotional will serve its readers by confirming what their spirit already knows: our sovereign God loves us completely and has good plans for us.
— Michelle Schaffer
Faith-Driven Leadership Mentor
OurKingdomAlliance.com

In these pages, you will encounter honest stories of hardship, but also the beautiful transformation that happens when someone chooses to receive the love of Jesus in the middle of it. This book

gently invites readers to see life through a different lens—one where pain is real, yet joy and peace are still possible.
— Kess Scharff
Author, Speaker, and Founder of SEEDS Ministry
KessScharff.com

"Jesus Laughs" offers something many people desperately need: the reminder that sorrow is not the end of the story. It points to a Savior who is present in our struggles and able to turn even difficult seasons into testimonies of grace.
— James Smith
Executive Director Chamber of Commerce KY
Linktr.ee/JamesDSmith

"Jesus Laughs" captures something we talk about often on the "Unlikely Housewives" Podcast—how God meets ordinary women in extraordinary ways. These reflections are honest, encouraging, and rooted in the truth that even in the middle of life's challenges, Jesus is present and working. It's the kind of devotional that reminds you God is not distant from your story—He's right in the middle of it.
— Tori Shirah & Tracy Stine
Hosts, "Unlikely Housewives" Podcast
UnlikelyHousewivesOfJoCo.com

The vulnerability and candid experiences shared in "Jesus Laughs" are both powerful and deeply relatable. These stories reminded me that even in life's most painful seasons, God is quietly working—shaping us and preparing something greater than we could imagine. This devotional is a beautiful encouragement for anyone who has walked through a low moment and needs to be reminded that God's plan always brings purpose and redemption.
— Katelyn Swiader, MS Ed, CCC-SLP
Speech-Language Pathologist & Voice and Communication Specialist
KatelynSwiader.com

"Jesus Laughs" beautifully reminds us that even life's most sour moments can hold unexpected sweetness when seen through God's perspective. The imagery of childlike faith—trusting enough to take another bite even when life tastes tart—was such a powerful reminder that God's presence transforms how we experience our circumstances. It stirred something in me to reflect on how often we brace for bitterness instead of expecting the deeper richness God may be cultivating. This book points us to a greater promise—the "Zoe life"—a life overflowing with joy, hope, and abundance in Christ. In a world that often feels heavy and cynical, this refreshing invitation to rediscover wonder, trust, and laughter with Jesus is exactly the message people are longing to hear right now.
— Rebekah Vasquez
Founder of Build His House Nonprofit
BuildHisHouse.com

Joy is not the absence of hardship—it is the evidence of faith that refuses to surrender in the middle of it. This devotional reminds readers that even in life's most difficult seasons, joy becomes the strength that carries us forward and anchors our hope in God.
— Dr. Tilda Whitaker-Bailey
D.Min. Hon, Founder & President Vision Christian University
VICU.info

Table of Contents

Introduction

His little face squished up and lips puckered with the first taste. My little waddler didn't cry as he sat in his high chair with an entire audience. Instead of fear, loneliness, confusion, or pain during a moment of what could have been isolation or intimidation, he instead witnessed the fulfillment of life-giving expressions from all those who love him. Watching in anticipation and hopefulness, we all stood laughing. So easily, in safety, instead of wincing, he joined in on the celebratory moment of joy and took another bite! In that precise frozen moment in time he experienced the totality of presence in an emotional, physical, mental, and spiritual blend (**Psalm 16:11[1] NIV**); what it feels like living and breathing on this side of Heaven. It wasn't just sweet, it was sour, but dwelling in the both/and, he was able to feel fully alive. And ready to take the next sour bite, in spite of its tart, unsavory flavor, because of the richness of experience that coincided with bitterness.

Adulting, on the contrary, doesn't often invite a cheering squad to the sour moments that lead us into wailing, working, or wallowing from the happenstance of life's lemons. But what if it could? What if we fixed our eyes on things above (**2 Corinthians 4:18[2] NIV**) and recognized Heaven's attention to every detail of our lives? Just as his father and I stood at our son's side, allowing the moment to

---

[1] **Psalm 16:11 (NIV)** – God's presence as fullness of joy
"You make known to me the path of life; you will fill me with joy in your presence, with eternal pleasures at your right hand."

[2] **2 Corinthians 4:18 (NIV)** – Fixing our eyes on the eternal
"So we fix our eyes not on what is seen, but on what is unseen … "

unfold, Abba stands with us, certain of our outcome. Not to harm us, but to invite us into a full-immersion experience that will forever change us. Eventually, through trust and safety, our learned behavior—like that of a child—becomes second nature, relishing the hope of the future and the laughter that springs from the sweetness the Lord planned for us all along. It seems simple in concept. But it requires a child-like faith (**Matthew 18:3[3] NIV**). It requires an eagerness and expectation beyond the first bite. It requires hope.

However, adding more requirements to the responsibilities already swirling around us can feel more like rigid religiosity and less like a sweet, restful invitation. So I think instead of prerequisites to living a joy-filled, laugh-instead-of-cry life, we will establish reference points. We'll use these reference points as developmental building blocks to our ultimate fulfillment—a promised *Zoe* life (*Zoe*, a Greek word meaning "life," appears multiple times throughout the Bible speaking to the rich, abundant life we are meant to experience with Jesus).

What is a *Zoe* life?

Sit with this sweet, sustaining opportunity:
A life of abundance. **John 10:10[4] (NIV)**
A life of full belief. **John 3:36[5] (NIV)**
A life of divinity. **2 Peter 1:3–4[6] (NIV)**

---

[3] **Matthew 18:3 (NIV)** – Childlike faith
" … unless you change and become like little children, you will never enter the kingdom of heaven."

[4] **John 10:10 (NIV)** – Abundant (*Zoe*) life
"I have come that they may have life, and have it to the full."

[5] **John 3:36 (NIV)** – Life through belief
"Whoever believes in the Son has eternal life…"

[6] **2 Peter 1:3–4 (NIV)** – Participation in divine nature
"…that you may participate in the divine nature…"

A life marked by joy, wonder, fullness and delight. **Romans 6:23**[7] **(NIV)**

It's a summer sun, sipping lemonade by the ocean kinda life.

This isn't just an idea or a far-off dream. It's often like an unopened gift we each have access to, yet leave sitting unnoticed in the corner—either through lack of understanding or simply because we fail to realize the gift has our name on it, penned by hand and secured by Heaven.

Unfortunately, the common trauma responses default to these soured states: sadness leading to grief (**Proverbs 13:12**[8] **NIV**), anger leading to bitterness (**Hebrews 12:15**[9] **NIV**), confusion leading to apathy, loneliness leading to isolation, cravings leading to addictions, and so on and so forth. The sugary sensation never seems to satisfy. And a dull, numbing pain lands on the heart and soul, leading to a less than appetizing experience that triggers insufficiency and lack. Eventually, our tastebuds become numb to the abundant promises from our kind, bountiful Father.

We console our emotions with the shortest and often quoted verse, "Jesus wept" (**John 11:35**[10] **NIV**), but our God is marked more by joy than He is by grief (**Zephaniah 3:17**[11] **NKJV; Hebrews**

---

[7] **Romans 6:23 (NIV)** – Eternal life as gift
"…the gift of God is eternal life in Christ Jesus our Lord."

[8] **Proverbs 13:12 (NIV)** – Hope deferred
"Hope deferred makes the heart sick … "

[9] **Hebrews 12:15 (NIV)** – Root of bitterness
" … that no bitter root grows up to cause trouble … "

[10] **John 11:35 (NIV)** – Jesus wept

[11] **Zephaniah 3:17 (NKJV)** – God rejoices with gladness
" … He will rejoice over you with gladness … "

12:11[12] **NIV**). So let's not use simple memorized scripture and common consolation language to dilute the entirety of the emotional wheel of Christ. The God who feels. The God who knows. The God who came as man to both experience and display every array of human existence. Let's remember: *Jesus Laughs.*

This is the very perspective shift that this book will lead you into. A bountiful, fruitful life awaits.

How?
Pre-requistes.

There were two key elements in that first bite of lemon with my son.

1. A divine set-up
2. A secure family

Can we agree that God has good plans for you (**Jeremiah 29:11**[13] **NIV**)? Predestined and arranged for your good and His glory (**Ephesians 1:11**[14] **NIV**)? I hope you're nodding your head earnestly, but I also know I've been on the "yah, yah I've heard it before" train. You know, the one that churchy verses don't stop you in your tracks anymore, but rather sound more like the Charlie Brown teacher ("wa wa wa … wa wa … wa wa"). Or perhaps even the thought of "good plans designed by a good God," or that "all things work together for good" (**Romans 8:28**[15] **NIV**), seems foreign because of the cycling mantras that nearly kept you from picking up this book in the first place.

---

[12] **Hebrews 12:11 (NIV)** – Discipline leading to joy and strength
  " … later on, however, it produces a harvest of righteousness and peace … "

[13] **Jeremiah 29:11 (NIV)** – God's good plans

[14] **Ephesians 1:11 (NIV)** – Predestined according to His will

[15] **Romans 8:28 (NIV)** – All things for good

Life isn't fair.
Life is hard.
It is what it is.
Welcome to the real world.
I can't catch a break.
I'm running on empty.
When it rains it pours.
I'm just surviving.
Expect nothing, you won't be disappointed.
Good things never last.

These are vendettas against the *Zoe* life. These word curses are constantly at work, souring our days and opposing the promises from Heaven, our fundamental truths. Tainted by the one who kills, steals, and destroys (**John 10:10**[16] **NIV**), these ideas are traps to keep you living below your gifted purpose and outside of your heavenly calling. This book is here to rewrite those ill-willed, wasted breaths into the life-giving *ruach* (Hebrew word meaning spirit, breath, or wind) that moves, empowers, and animates all creation—especially YOU.

There is a divine setup in your life, and every sour circumstance has a sweet opportunity for lasting fruitfulness (**John 15:2**[17] **NIV**), not just for you, but for all of those around you. But if you harvest the fruit too soon, it won't yield the same sweetness. Maturity is vital (**James 1:2–4**[18] **NIV**). And this resource will be a key to unlock the layers of Truth to sustain that freedom fully and completely— though of course only perfectly through Him—not by our flesh or knowledge alone, but by His Spirit.

And what is even more beautiful about the text to come, is it couldn't be done without the sisterhood gathered here. A repre-

---

[16] **John 10:10 (NIV)** – Thief comes to steal, kill, destroy

[17] **John 15:2 (NIV)** – Pruning for fruitfulness

[18] **James 1:2–4 (NIV)** – Trials producing maturity

sentation of the same gathering that stood before Cooper, my son, with his first taste of lemon. The same gathering that joined in on your grand entrance to this world. The same ones who witnessed the loss, devastation, pain, and torment and who wills you into finding the sweetness that has been there all along. A place where you can find safety and assurance. A place to walk out of the orphan spirit and into the understanding of your adoption (**Romans 8:15**[19] **NIV; Galatians 4:5–7**[20] **NIV**) into the family of God. This prerequisite can feel impossible when your exposure to broken relationships has been your norm, but even as Jesus was rejected in His hometown, there was a family, a mother, a father, brothers and sisters, that welcomed Him … and we are waiting for you, too (**Ephesians 2:19**[21] **NIV**). Arms wide open. With a ring and a robe to welcome you into the overflowing house full of the Father's laughter (**Luke 15:20–24**[22] **NIV**).

So as you venture through these lemonade concoctions of Heaven from each of the "sweet" authors, you won't see a lack of vulnerability, you won't gag from perfection, and you won't thirst for more of their words. Instead, you'll be summoned into the lemonade life, filled with the succulent Word of God—just a sweet surrender away (**Jeremiah 15:16**[23] **NIV**).

We don't hold His Word lightly. As you can see in this introduction alone, we take it in context and simmer with it, season by season. As God teaches us the wonderful ingredients that can turn what may at first appear to be sour into sweet, we have His sustaining Truth to yield a bountiful blessing. So don't be a passerby of Eden's

---

[19] **Romans 8:15 (NIV)** – Spirit of adoption

[20] **Galatians 4:5–7 (NIV)** – Sons and daughters, not slaves

[21] **Galatians 4:5–7 (NIV)** – Sons and daughters, not slaves

[22] **Luke 15:20–24 (NIV)** – Robe, ring, restoration

[23] **Jeremiah 15:16 (NIV)** – God's Word as joy

garden of delight … pause, reflect, notice the wisdom being shared in every chapter, and apply His Word as the healing, heavenly hope to quench your soul.

Repenting (**Acts 3:19**[24] **NIV**) and walking out of the orphan spirit and into family is changing how we live. After all, we are adopted, a new creation (**2 Corinthians 5:17**[25] **NIV**). And that invitation is the sweetest gift that accompanies all of the Truths, displaces all of the lies, and seals your identity alongside Jesus (**Colossians 3:3–4**[26] **NIV**). The One who laughs. The One whose existence is marked by joy. The One who gifts us the *Zoe* life of abundance. On the other side of this river of testimonies—where sour turns to sweet—is the land of milk and honey. Come indulge and delight with us and the Father (**Psalm 119:103**[27] **NIV**).

And as a supportive reflective tool, get your journal ready so you, too, can chuckle with Jesus over your own lemon-wincing moments of life. You won't regret taking the next step to satisfy your thirst with Scripture, either. These verses are meant to be the very seeds to produce the sweetness marking your life as sacred.

---

[24] **Acts 3:19 (NIV)** – Repentance brings refreshing

[25] **2 Corinthians 5:17 (NIV)** – New creation

[26] **Colossians 3:3–4 (NIV)** – Life hidden with Christ

[27] **Psalm 119:103 (NIV)** – Sweeter than honey

The Lemon Shake Up

Grace in the Mess and Strength in the Sour

| Nicky Asher-Bowling |

"Each time he said, 'My grace is all you need. My power works best in weakness.'"
2 Corinthians 12:9 NLT

Chapter 1

The boys and I had come home from church on a Sunday. I fed them lunch, and they played in the living room while watching a cartoon VHS tape on an old 30-inch tube TV a friend of my ex-husband had given me long ago. I was lying on the couch resting and watching them play, when I fell asleep. As I slept, I heard something running and thumping. When I woke up, I saw our dog, Shelby, chasing a small white "ball" from our kitchen into the living room. At first I didn't think anything of it until I saw her smash it. I realized it was an egg. I jumped up and ran into the kitchen to see my youngest boy, who was around 2 years old, standing in the middle of the floor with dozens of smashed eggs on the floor. The floor was a huge snotty mess! I yelled at him to get out of the kitchen, but he slid all over and couldn't stand on his own. I picked him up, took his clothes off, and got bath towels to clean up the kitchen floor. The entire floor was covered. It was the biggest mess of eggs I had ever seen! Cleaning the floor took me forever—I mean, for-ever. I was so mad. Why did I fall asleep? Why did I have so many eggs in the fridge? Why did this toddler keep coming into the kitchen while I was trying to clean up this nasty, goopy mess he made? I called my mom for advice, sympathy, something, and she laughed hilariously! I mean, do you blame her? In that moment, I didn't want anyone to laugh. I wanted to know why I reacted with anger.

God has understood my nature from the very beginning, long before I completely understood it. He knew I was an introvert; He knew I kept everything neatly bottled up inside; and He knew at this point in my life—newly divorced—I was so stressed from carrying all my burdens. I had not been laying them at His feet like these broken eggs. If only I had thrown my broken eggs down for Him to pick up and put back together, my life in that moment would have been so much easier. But I hadn't learned how to give it over to Jesus yet. Yes, I grew up in faith, but I had never practiced it. I internalized everything in my life.

At this point, I hadn't been diagnosed with bipolar disorder. So I didn't understand why, after marriage, motherhood, and divorce, I was exploding?

"Each time he said, 'My grace is all you need. My power works best in weakness.'" 2 Corinthians 12:9 (NLT) says it best that God works best when we are weak, but we have to let Him work in our lives. Paul had an illness that He had been asking God to remove from His life. God didn't ignore his request for healing; instead He told him, my grace is sufficient for you. God has more than enough grace for us, it's there for us. When we let Him work in our life during our weakest point, His grace is all we need. What I really didn't understand is the excruciating emotional pain I had endured. I still had to go through them; I had to experience them to learn from them. I felt God should have taken the pain away. I had never experienced this before I found out my husband—whom I worshipped and was so in love with—had been unfaithful to me. This was a pain that broke my heart and left me completely bereft. God's grace helps us endure those pains and injustices we feel; He's there with us. He allows them so we can get stronger and draw closer to Him. I wished I knew this lesson long ago, but God knew I had to learn from my mistakes even if I had to rinse and repeat over and over again. Thank goodness, He's faithful to us! Even as I'm learning from my mistakes, this will be something I will have to help my sons with in the future.

After a long day at work, on a sunny, breezy afternoon, I got an unexpected phone call from my middle son. And immediately I knew—this was not a "just checking in" call. Of all my sons, my middle one was the responsible one. The reliable one. The one who usually called *me* to remind *me* of things. So when I saw his name pop up, my stomach dropped.

I answered, "Hey, what's up, Bub?" And then he casually and very calmly explained that he had been playing with paper on his windowsill … and lighting it on fire. Because obviously. The wind, apparently feeling left out, grabbed the flaming paper, blew it into the bedroom, onto the carpet, and—surprise—the carpet caught fire. I knew it was serious because I heard it in his voice. Fear. Real fear. He was scared. My first thought wasn't anger. It was, "Are you okay? Are you burned?" He had asthma, so I was already picturing smoke, ER visits, and panic attacks. He said, "No, I'm fine. I just thought I wasn't going to be able to put it out." Oh. *Just that.* I asked, "Do you need me to come home?" He said, "No … you'll see it when you get home. The fire's out. I promise."

And that's when the *other* thought kicked in: Why on earth were you playing with fire … with the window open? Now, once a parent realizes their child is safe, there's usually a shift. Fear steps aside … and anger pulls up a chair. And let me tell you—I already had anger issues. I had been diagnosed with bipolar disorder by then, and while I was on medication, it wasn't exactly under control. It was more like … *barely supervised.*

I worried constantly about my kids. My stress level lived at 10. I was terrified they wouldn't grow up to be responsible adults. I come from a family with a history of petty crime and addiction, and that fear sat in the back of my mind all the time: *What if my kids end up there, too?* That fear took me straight back to my childhood— when my brother, about the same age as my son, broke into a Victorian house across the street with some friends. They played with fire, too. They burned the entire house down. The older kid ran, because he knew jail was waiting. My brother wasn't old enough, so he went to juvenile detention, then probation, then therapy he hated. That whole mess stuck with me. So when my son told me he'd been playing with fire, it hit *everything* at once. Fear. Anger. Guilt. I felt like I'd failed—failed at teaching right from wrong, failed at protecting him, failed at parenting altogether.

What I didn't understand yet—what I hadn't learned—was that mistakes are unavoidable. You can't grow without them.

> *"Consider it pure joy, my brothers and sisters,*
> *whenever you face trials of many kinds, because*
> *you know that the testing of your faith produces*
> *perseverance."*
> *(James 1:2—3, NIV)*

You can't learn from someone else's experience—you have to live your own. Now? We laugh about it. The fire burned a nice big hole in the carpet, and my son tried to hide it by keeping something over it … permanently. Like, very casually pretending it wasn't there. It reminded me that I could teach my kids. I could guide them. I could warn them until I was blue in the face. But ultimately, *they* chose.

And honestly? So do we. In my Christian walk, I used to think following God meant He would remove the bad stuff. The pain. The mess. The fires—literal or figurative. But the bad stuff doesn't go away. What changes is how we respond. How we lean on God *in* it.

God doesn't promise a fire-free life. He promises presence.

That's when I began to understand this verse differently: "My grace is all you need. My power works best in weakness" (2 Corinthians 12:9, NLT). God doesn't promise a fire-free life. He promises presence.

Looking back now, I can see how protected we were. That situation could have been *so much worse.* And while the bad still happened, the worst didn't. God had angels camped around us then—and He still does now. Around me. Around you. The bad may still happen. But the worst? God, in His grace, often keeps that from ever touching us. And that is something worth trusting.

When I was first married, my husband wasn't ready to have children. We had been married about a year, and I desperately wanted a baby. I knew how he felt—afraid and not ready—but I was ready. I had been praying about it.

At the time, our church was in the middle of a revival. A minister with the gift of prophecy was preaching. He would come over to someone, prophesy, and reveal something deeply personal—right there in front of everyone, with a microphone. I don't know if you've ever experienced that, but I was scared of him. I was still very much an introvert. The thought of someone praying over me publicly terrified me. Yet I had been praying for a secret request from God. I hadn't even told my husband I was asking God for a baby.

One night, toward the end of the revival, the minister stopped and said, "There is a young woman here who has been praying to have a baby." My heart sank. I felt sick to my stomach. When he said it, I knew it was me. And I also knew that when God calls you to step out in faith for your heart's desire, you have to move. He said it once. No one responded. He said it again.

I could not stay in my seat. I don't know what would have happened if I hadn't stepped out. Maybe I would have gotten pregnant later. Maybe I wouldn't have. I truly don't know. But in that moment, I knew I had to choose faith. So I stepped into the aisle. I was shaking. I was nervous. I was putting myself in the spotlight I had avoided my entire life. But I went.

He prayed over me and said, "If you want God to answer your prayer, hold your arms out like you're holding a baby." I did. He laid his jacket across my arms, placed his hands on me, and prayed. And I felt God's Spirit fill me.

At that moment, I knew—no matter what happened—God had heard me. I stood there, praying, rocking that jacket like a baby in my arms. When I finished, I handed it back to him.

It was one of the bravest moments of my life. Nine months later, I gave birth to our first son. He was a delight—and very challenging, to say the least. But that night gave me boldness. It marked the beginning of something in me changing. It marked the beginning of something changing inside of me. I was thinking of someone other than myself, a little someone who would be dependent on me.

Motherhood forced me out of my shell. I learned quickly that if you don't stand up for your children, no one else will.

My firstborn was eventually diagnosed with schizoaffective disorder. The simplest way to describe it is a combination of bipolar disorder and hallucinations. He began showing symptoms around 9 or 10 years old. At first, I thought he just had an active imagination. Many children have imaginary friends. But his symptoms didn't fade.

Even earlier, around age 3, he showed behaviors that mimicked ADHD. When he started school, he struggled to concentrate and sit still. Doctors treated him for ADHD, but the medications didn't help because ADHD wasn't the root issue. In the medical system, children under 18 are rarely diagnosed with schizoaffective disorder. So his psychiatrist documented ADHD for insurance purposes, while treating the symptoms appropriately.

Raising him was incredibly challenging. I had to learn to advocate for him. I had to find my voice.

There were times the school wanted to isolate him or restrain him if he became overwhelmed. They asked for permission to physically tie him down and remove him from class if necessary. I was horrified. They did not understand my son. He was not violent. He struggled with focus and emotional regulation, not aggression.

Eventually, I moved him to a smaller rural school district where he could receive more individualized attention. He entered a structured program with clear routines and strict guidelines—but one that was consistent and supportive. In that environment, he flourished. They taught him life skills along with academics, and it made all the difference.

Even though I had stepped away from church during that season, I still felt God leading me. He used my son's challenges to develop strength in me—to ground me in conviction and courage.

As an adult, my son continued living with us for several years. Many traditional medications used for hallucinations left him in a near-zombie state. I attended appointments with him and constantly asked, "Is this the best option for him?"

Eventually, his psychiatrist recommended a newer medication with promising research results. Once it received FDA approval, he started taking it. The change was dramatic. He came out of the fog. He became alert, engaged, and present. For the first time, he could carry conversations consistently. Before that, he had struggled with insomnia, going days without sleep, forgetting to eat, drink, or shower. Daily functioning was nearly impossible.

With the new treatment, we began preparing him for independence. Around age 29 or 30, he decided he wanted to live on his own. He was excited—and understandably nervous. We worked together on budgeting, cooking, cleaning, and daily routines. Because he wasn't able to work, we focused on life skills and stability. Today, he lives independently.

When life hands you lemons, they taste bitter. You don't understand why it's happening. You question God. You question yourself. But trusting that God is walking with you—even when you don't see the outcome—is what carries you through.

There were seasons when I felt abandoned, confused, and exhausted. But looking back, I see His hand in every step. If God had not been guarding us, protecting us, strengthening us, how much worse could it have been?

Even now, I still experience anxiety and depression. Life doesn't suddenly become perfect. But I can always find evidence of God's faithfulness. I have seen Him reach down into my darkest places and remind me I am not alone. That is grace. When life gives you a lemon, don't throw it away. Hold it. Thank God for it—even if you don't understand it yet.

I'm reminded of when I used to walk the Rose Festival with my grandmother, my sister, and my cousins, visiting vendors and laughing together. My hometown, known as the City of Roses, celebrated with booths lining the promenade and local businesses filling the streets. Our church sold elephant ears, funnel cakes, and lemon shakeups. I loved those lemon shakeups. How do you turn something sour into something sweet and refreshing? You shake it. You add sugar. You transform it. That's exactly what God does.

The very thing that feels sharp and bitter becomes the ingredient for something beautiful. The miracle often comes wrapped inside the hardship. Even now, when I think about the hardest seasons of my life, I see the sweetness that came later. God took what felt unbearable and used it to strengthen me, deepen my faith, and teach me how to manage my anxiety and depression. Remember this: The lemons in your life can become a lemon shakeup. Sweet. Refreshing. Life-giving. One day, you'll look back and see what God was doing while you were walking through the bitter season. And you'll taste the sweetness.

The mess isn't the miracle. What God does with it is.

At the Rose Festival, they'd take a sharp lemon, add sugar, put a lid on it, and shake it until it changed. That's what God has done with my life. He didn't remove the eggs. He didn't stop the fire. He didn't prevent the diagnosis. But He added grace. He added strength. And He shook me into something sweeter.

The mess isn't the miracle. What God does with it is.

I've learned this much: When life hands you lemons, don't panic. Don't light them on fire. And definitely don't slip on the eggs. Just add some sugar … and shake.

The *Lemonade*

| I've learned this much: When life hands you lemons, don't panic. Don't light them on fire. And definitely don't slip on the eggs. Just add some sugar ... and shake. |

Where might God be adding "sugar" in your life that you're too focused on the sour to taste?

What "lemons" in your life have you been resenting instead of allowing God to use?

"Each time he said, 'My grace is all you need. My power works best in weakness.'"
2 Corinthians 12:9 NLT

| Meet Nicky Asher-Bowling |

Nicky Asher-Bowling is a Christian mental health coach, podcaster, and writer who is still very much learning as she goes. She hosts "It's Going to Be Okay!" where she talks honestly about depression, anxiety, faith, family, and the moments when life doesn't turn out the way you prayed it would.

Drawing from lived experience, coaching work, and a lot of grace, Nicky writes for women who love Jesus but don't have it all figured out. She believes faith can be sincere, healing can be slow, and sometimes the most spiritual response is realizing Jesus is probably shaking His head—and smiling—at the situation.

The Joy I Didn't Know was Mine

God doesn't just sweeten lemons, He asks for the pitcher

| Melissa Batt |

"You have turned my mourning into joyful dancing. You have taken away my clothes of mourning and clothed me with joy, that I might sing praises to you and not be silent. Oh Lord my God, I will give you thanks forever!"
Psalm 30:11-12 NLT

Chapter 2

Additional reading: All of Psalm 30; 1 Chronicles 21

King David was a humble man lovingly known as "a man after God's own heart." While not perfect, when pointed out to him, he was quick to acknowledge the errors of his ways.

In Psalm 30 and 1 Chronicles 21, David is faced with the consequences of his pride and misalignment with the Lord after requesting a census to be taken of all the fighting men in Israel.

Terrified of choices he never wanted to make, feeling the weight of his sins, David is left with nowhere to hide and nobody to blame but himself. Like us, when his reality magnified his fear, he had a choice to make. He could acknowledge his mistake, surrender his sin, and cry out to God for help, or he could dismiss everything and attempt to avoid what was hard. Thankfully, he was desperate enough to cry out for help and choose repentance.

In Psalm 30, as we read the words of the song David wrote, we can easily recognize his heart of gratitude. He is thanking God for lifting him up from the pit of death instead of allowing him to be overcome by it. I often recognize my own *pit* experiences and self-inflicted struggles.

There was a time when I knew God had asked me to do something, and while I didn't fully understand it, without even considering the repercussions, I immediately said *NO. I didn't doubt that it was God; I just didn't fully understand why He would ask.* I dismissed it so quickly that it would be years before I would even realize that the struggle and pain I was enduring was not at the fault of someone else, but instead, it was all me. My crummy circumstances were the clear consequences of my own misalignment, pride, and disobedience.

Like David in 1 Chronicles 21:26 when he built an altar to the Lord and sacrificed both burnt offerings and fellowship offerings, I didn't just need relief from the trouble. I also needed fellowship and peace with the Lord, along with the restoration of my joy.

Bible commentator Matthew Henry, in "Matthew Henry's Concise Commentary on the Whole Bible," describes the altar God commanded David to build as "a blessed token of reconciliation," reminding us that even in the aftermath of failure, God still provides a way back to Him. Henry also points to the greater picture of redemption, reminding us that through Jesus Christ, we are not met with a consuming fire but with a reconciled God.

So repenting I did. And yet, it didn't immediately erase the pit. Instead, it opened the door to healing.

For David, the pit meant facing the consequences of his sin. For me, it showed up as depression. I think the pit shows up differently for each of us, but we will always find this true: It moves us into a position of surrender and leaves us in desperate need of a rescue.

In that season, the sour I felt wasn't just circumstantial. It wasn't just *a thought* I could reframe. Instead, it seemed to consume my entire life, including my body and nervous system.

For me, depression rarely shows up dramatically. Instead, it kind of sneaks in subtly, like a lazy day that just won't leave. It feels like zero energy and no capacity to do anything productive. It looks like binge-watching "The Real Housewives of Orange County" or doing anything and everything I can to numb out and escape my real life.

I remember the first time someone asked me if I was depressed. I was pregnant with my third baby, and my mom asked. It was the beginning of a long season, and it wouldn't be the only time the question came up.

At the time, I believed depression looked like it was portrayed on television and in the movies, sitting in a corner in a dark room, crying all day, wanting to end one's life. I was too numb to cry and didn't want to end my life; I just wanted to go to sleep and wake up when it got better.

I shrugged her off, dismissed her concern with an eye roll, and said, *Nooo … I'm not depressed. Why would you even think that?*

The truth is, she knew because she had also lived it. I now understand how most of what I experienced as a child was the result of having parents with their own mental health struggles.

It wouldn't be much longer before more signs would start revealing themselves. What started with wanting to escape and read books all day soon turned into panic attacks, visits to see a therapist, and a prescription for an antidepressant.

Joy felt so nonexistent in those days that I didn't even recognize that it was possible or even missing in my life. Laughter felt fake. I felt numb and lethargic. And if I had any hope at all, it had me wishing for someday instead of being where my feet were, living in the moment of the present day. I didn't realize it at the time, but that lack of joy had a long history.

A few years ago, I went through a group coaching exercise where we were each asked to answer a simple question: What was our earliest childhood memory of having fun?

Of all the questions that would get me stuck, I would have never imagined it being that one. Yet, there I was, for the first time in my mid-30s, recognizing the truth of my childhood, unable to answer.

I couldn't think of a single memory of myself laughing, feeling carefree, or experiencing the joys of being a child. And the truth is, I'm an '80s baby whose childhood was well-documented. I looked through photo albums, watched home videos, and sadly, what I saw was a child who was extra cautious, always nervous, and questioning everything and everyone.

As harsh as it sounds, I didn't grow up feeling safe. From an early age, my lived experiences taught me that I couldn't rely on anyone and chaos would be around the corner. I believed the only person I could trust was *me, myself, and I*. And, often, I felt responsible to help everyone else, including those who were supposed to help me. It felt wiser to hide from the world than to allow myself to be open and exposed to it. Before I had language for fear, I had already learned control.

Looking back now, this was an early season of lots of lemons dropped into my life. And through them, the lie I began to believe was quietly forming in my mind:

Relying on myself was my only option.

Long before I knew God, even as a child, I was already learning how to survive the sour. It would be years before I would learn that sweetness even existed or that it was meant for me.

As someone who has gone through life with childhood trauma and seasons of anxiety, depression, and postpartum depression, I am *ultra* familiar with the pit of despair.

Throughout the years, I have to admit I have tried to sweeten my life in all the ways I knew how.

Ask anyone who knows me, and they will tell you that I'm a high-achieving, top-performing, control freak who is passionate about helping others. If I'm going to do it, I'm going to do it all the way, and it's going to be good. Failure is not an option. People depend on me.

Looking back, I can see how "doing it all the way" protected me from the emotions that came with people letting me down. If I were to fail, I would be letting myself down. Success gave me a sense of control, and even when life began *life-ing*, and things fell apart, it felt safer knowing I was the one in charge. And when I was caring for others and protecting those I loved, I neglected myself.

Control was behind every *imitation* sweetener I chose. It didn't remove the sour taste, though. It only made it more tolerable for a short time. Like all imitations, it only lasts so long and works only until it doesn't.

Control was behind every imitation sweetener I chose.

By my 30s, I fully believed in God and genuinely felt like I was living a surrendered life. But the truth is that life was happening so fast that I didn't yet recognize the areas where I was operating from the old wounds of brokenness. These wounds created bad habits, and they don't go away unless we do it on purpose.

Control eventually cost me my health, and when my health began to suffer, productivity followed. I was forced to slow down, and it was there in the quiet that I began to hear the Holy Spirit tell me to listen and pay attention.

Looking back, I don't think control started as pride. Instead, I think as a child, it was a way to protect myself emotionally. But even what felt like wisdom can quietly turn to pride.

And when the control was threatened, fear, anxiety, and overwhelm came rushing in.

The irony isn't lost on me that I have often described myself as "the girl who is afraid of everything." Both fear and anxiety have been ongoing stumbling blocks for me, and I've learned there's a direct connection between them and my struggle to give up control.

When my eyes are fixed on myself or someone else and I am striving to achieve in my own strength, fear, worry, and anxiety will always consume me.

But when my eyes are fixed on the Lord, my faith sustains me, and I can operate with bold courage. Life begins to feel safe, not because I'm in control but because I've learned to trust who is carrying it for me.

For years, I was trying to fix the sour on my own. I was gripping the pitcher of lemons so tightly that I never stopped to ask if it was mine to carry in the first place.

Little moments of breakthrough came once I stopped managing the pain, settling for the imitations, and finally invited God into it.

The breakthrough didn't come from perfect effort. It came from loosening my grip and slowly placing the pitcher in His hands.

God has me on a mission of slowly, and sometimes painfully, undoing what I picked up as bad habits, one baby step at a time. It's a messy process, especially when surviving shaped habits before I ever knew there was another way.

It began with learning to pay attention to my body.

Facial swelling was the first sign. It looked like an allergic reaction to something and turned into lots of emergency room visits. I finally recognized the connection to overworking and lack of sleep, and instead of pushing through, God began teaching me how to rest properly. I had no idea that resting was God's will and that science and Scripture both speak to how productive active rest can be for us.

He began helping me see how I treated myself differently from how I treated others and encouraged me to start honoring my body, as it is truly something to lovingly care for.

He also helped me start paying attention to what I ate and how it made me feel. I learned to start surrendering my stress and emotions instead of stuffing them down with ice cream and chocolate. Food became something to support and nourish my body the way He designed it.

Life is messy, friend. Bad things happen. And it seems like in life we tend to do one of two things. We focus solely on the hard, bad things that have happened and allow ourselves to remain in full victim mode and live in self-pity, or we do the complete opposite and pretend the hard things never happened. Instead, we bury it deep inside and move along with our day, avoiding the heartache.

But God has shown me a different way.

God has taught me one baby step at a time that healing isn't always these grandiose moments we think they should be. Sometimes it comes in everyday moments of slowing down, paying attention, and letting Jesus into the everyday moments of life.

For me, sweetness didn't arrive the way I thought it would. And yet, it still showed up abundantly, and in places I never expected.

Trying something new for me looked like using a chainsaw for the first time, playing laser tag with the kids instead of just watching or scrolling until they were done, and driving myself to my hometown and crossing the bridge that once terrified me.

As joy and gladness slowly began showing up in these ordinary ways, God continued to invite me to go deeper.

It doesn't mean "everything is fixed," and we sing "Kumbaya" and call it all done. But it does mean living in the moment, being intentional, and allowing ourselves to experience excitement and feel alive as we remain sensitive to the Holy Spirit and say yes to the journey God has us on.

Each day, I continue to learn to trust Him more as He continues to challenge me to let go of control and follow Him.

Today, I get to experience life with a childlike wonder and curiosity in ways I never did as a child. I'm proof that He will make all things good, restore what is lost, and redeem all things we once believed were broken.

There's a way that neither denies nor ignores the pain and also doesn't glorify or idolize it. God wants our grief to be honest and surrendered, not dismissed flippantly or worn as a badge of honor. It's not one or the other. We can acknowledge the pain AND surrender it honestly.

He calls us to come to Him when we become misaligned and to abide in Him. Remaining connected to the vine, He continues to heal, restore, and set us free as we go about our Father's business to carry out His holy work. Sometimes this also means turning from the old ways and repenting from what we didn't even know was wrong. He knows, He cares, and He loves us deeply and wants what is best for us.

Because Jesus lives, we do not have to remain broken. He heals the brokenhearted, and it's His desire for each of us to experience the fullness of life, including the experience of full JOY.

Life was never intended to be this hard and heavy. Sometimes, like David, we get ourselves mixed up and suffer consequences because of poor decisions and misalignment. Even then, God lovingly redirects us to a place of repentance and restoration. Other times, the suffering comes at no fault of our own, through wounds we didn't choose, trauma we didn't invite, and circumstances we couldn't control.

And if we are honest, most of us live somewhere in between those realities because we live in a fallen world and are prone to messing up and operating out of our own flesh.

The good news, though, is that no matter the source of our suffering, God delights in meeting us right where we are. We just have to invite Him in and hand Him our pitcher. So the question becomes this:

Will we give Him our pitcher and let Him add the real sweetness, instead of settling for imitations?

Maybe it's time to stop trying so hard to fix yourself, and instead notice where you've been trying to manage the sour and harsh bitterness of your life on your own.

Know this. Lamenting is necessary. It's biblical and a command. Grieve well, my friend. Mourn what was lost. Bring all of your sorrows to God without prettying them up first or trying to be overly spiritual. He sees the mess and even knows the words you want to say, even when you don't want to say them out loud. Wail if you need to, scream at Him if you must. Get it out of your head so you can let Jesus into that part of your heart. He will meet you just as you are, right where you are.

And good news, also. You don't have to stay there. Weeping may endure for the night, but His JOY comes in the morning (Psalm 30:5, NKJV). Jesus invites you to let Him in to restore and redeem. He wants to add the sweetness into your life that you will never be able to replicate on your own. He desires for you to truly experience belly laughs and freedom, whether again or for the very first time. Never forget that God meets us right where we are and will never fail us. We can stand on His promises in His Word.

The Lemonade

| Real sweetness comes when we
stop settling for imitations and give
Him our pitcher. |

Think about a loss, disappointment, or painful season you have tried to move past without fully acknowledging. What emotions have you been carrying? What would it look like to bring that grief honestly before God and allow Him to meet you there?

Sometimes we try to make difficult things more manageable by staying busy, staying in control, or relying only on ourselves. Where might you be doing this in your life right now? What might change if you invited God into that place instead of managing it on your own?

"You have turned my mourning into joyful dancing. You have taken away my clothes of mourning and clothed me with joy, that I might sing praises to you and not be silent. Oh Lord my God, I will give you thanks forever!"
Psalm 30:11-12 NLT

| Meet Melissa Batt |

Melissa Batt is a Christian life coach, speaker, and podcast host who helps women move out of overwhelm and survival mode by learning how to surrender what was never theirs to carry. She hosts the "God-Sized Dreams" podcast and has appeared in multiple magazines, podcast, radio, and television interviews addressing faith, mental health, and personal growth.

Through her own journey with trauma, anxiety, and burnout, Melissa offers compassionate, faith-centered insight rooted in lived experience. Her work focuses on helping women find freedom, clarity, and joy through trust, surrender, and intentional living.

The Scenic Route Turned Divine

The Puckered Pain

| Melody Ganaway |

*"No discipline seems pleasant at the time,
but painful. Later on, however, it
produces a harvest of righteousness
and peace for those who
have been trained by it."*
Hebrews 12:11 NIV

Chapter 3

I grew up always believing I could do anything. I was taught to live without fear. As early as 2 years old, my parents would let me walk around the mall and talk to strangers. They would walk 10 feet behind me and just let me explore. This was my happy place because deep inside as early as I can remember, I knew God wanted me to be a performer onstage. My parents always encouraged me to sing and dance for anyone who would listen: the neighborhood civic league meeting, my relatives at the reunion, the local talent show. At home, I would pop the VHS tape into the video recorder and put on full productions with my little brother. I was always comfortable in front of any audience.

The world was my home. I felt safe to explore and seek adventure wherever I would roam. As I got older, Shakespeare's words, "All the world's a stage … " became my motto, and I set out to conquer my dreams in the Big Apple—New York City! Go big or go home! I traveled all over the world performing on some of the biggest stages with the largest companies in the world. I worked with children's theatre companies where we brought theatre to underserved communities that didn't have access to these types of programs. I loved giving audiences an opportunity to escape and witness the most beautiful stories ever told. I was living my dream, or so I thought. The more I performed professionally, the more I began to feel as though I was running on empty.

Growing up in the theatre, I always connected self-worth to my success. This felt normal to me. I would measure my happiness based on how many musicals I was in, how many lines I had, how many people were at my performances, how loud they would cheer, etc. This felt right. This made me feel whole. But as I got older, I realized I was on a race track that would never end, watching the gas gauge getting closer and closer to E. I was going in circles seeking this validation. The moment I felt empty or rather not good enough, I would book the next show or find the next audience.

I remember finishing out two sold out weekends at Madison Square Garden in NYC where we had performed for around 80,000 people. Thoughts began flooding my mind. *What's next? Am I enough now? If so, why do I feel so unfulfilled? If God gave me this purpose then why do I feel like I'm letting Him down?* The pressure started to get to me; I second guessed myself constantly, wondering if I would remember the lines when I walked out onto the stage. I thought the war was with myself, but when I looked deeper, I realized the war was really with God.

"But seek first the kingdom of God and his righteousness, and all these things will be added to you" (Matthew 6:33, ESV). However, I thought my way was better. I placed God safely in His box. You know, the one where we conveniently pick and choose what suits our life best? I spent time with Him on Sundays when I would worship, I thanked Him when something successfully happened, or prayed to Him when I needed Him. As Natalie Grant says in her song "King of the World," I had fit Him "in the walls inside my mind," I put Him in the "box that I've designed." I was completely convinced I knew the better way. Little did I know, I was in for a rude awakening.

I went off tour and found a cute little theme park for kids in Pennsylvania's Amish Country. Naturally, this would be better. Maybe smaller audiences would mean less pressure. Nope, I felt worse. I felt bored and lonely. I didn't really get along with many of my cast members. We had different interests. It felt like a job, no longer something I was inspired to do. So, what does one do when they need excitement in their life?

Online dating.

Yep, I believed in the fairytales. I grew up in the world of Disney princesses. I wanted to be saved by my prince. This would make my inner child happier, right? I didn't receive the validation I needed from large or small audiences, so maybe then a guy would make me feel better. The only problem was I hadn't had much luck with relationships in the past. I always picked my career over love, but perhaps I was destined to find the man of my dreams in the middle of nowhere. I read every self-help book thinking this would cure my curse of bad relationships. Turns out it wasn't fun or dreamy like the fairytales talk about. Each partner became a mirror into my soul exposing the deepest parts of me that I was not ready to fix or address; the parts I thought I could ignore or run away from with shiny lights and loud cheers.

Suddenly, as I dated more and more, I realized now why performing didn't fulfill me, why I still felt empty when the ghost light[28] would ignite. Deep down, I didn't love myself. I needed someone else to look into the mirror—I couldn't bear to see myself. I needed men to validate a version of myself that I actually hated, and this was eating away at my very being. It prohibited me from truly healing and being the best version of myself. And yet, it felt easier to skip the work. What if I didn't love this new, different version of myself? What if I hated it even more? The truth was that this current, unhealed version of myself was at least more bearable to face because it was familiar. It was me.

------

[28] A ghostlight (or ghost light) is a single, electric lamp left burning on an empty theatre stage, usually overnight, for safety, practicality, and superstition.

So I jumped into another unhealthy relationship, but this time it wouldn't just wear on my emotions. It began to impact my health. I started breaking out into horrible rashes all over my body. It was so embarrassing. As a performer, I had to keep it a secret and used makeup to cover it up. I couldn't let anyone see my weakness and had to make sure I looked the part. I took medication as a bandaid to stop the pain, but it continued, and when I tried to mask it, it only got worse.

One night, my cast and I were having a little party over at the house where we were all staying. Everyone was listening to music, playing games and drinking. One of the cast members and I hadn't had the best relationship. For one reason or another, our personalities didn't click. I've always been a people pleaser so I didn't take to this dynamic very well. We were all sitting around and he went to look for something in a bag for the game. Accidentally, he reached into my bag and pulled out my medication for my rashes. Before I could say anything, he started laughing and yelling to everyone, "Melody has STDs! Wow, Melody, I didn't know that you have STDs!" Horrified, I froze. They began to laugh or stare. No one cared enough to question it or stand up for me. I was the butt of the joke. I had never felt so alone in my whole life. I didn't know what to say or do, except run away before they could see me cry. I was ashamed of this imperfection, the dark piece of myself I had been battling but couldn't fix or heal. I immediately grabbed my bag and ran outside to the park to sob. Never in my life had I cried so deeply. All of the feelings of never being good enough, always seeking validation I didn't get, and never being truly seen hit me harder than I ever imagined. I was betrayed, I was abandoned. All of the trauma I felt from my past became present again, heavy like a weight, smothering me. My worst nightmare hadn't just physicalized in my body, but now was exposed to everyone. I cried to God to help me. My mind and body were screaming for help, but I had chosen to ignore it for so long. I wept and wept until I was numb. I knew that at that moment I had to surrender. My way was no longer the right way. I couldn't fix my life, my health, my soul without God. So I prayed harder than I had ever prayed before. I sat in complete silence with Him and asked Him to show me the way. I meditated and His verses began to inspire me: "These things I have spoken to you, that in Me you may have peace. In the world, you will have tribulation: but be of good cheer. I have overcome the world" (John 16:33, NKJV). I needed to stop seeking validation from the world and live for Him.

I needed to stop seeking validation from the world and live for Him.

There was only one thing for me to do. I left at the end of my contract and moved home. I needed a break from the theatre industry that was fueling this need for worldly validation. I moved in with my parents so I could remember who I was at my core and be around the people who love me for just existing. No matter what path I drifted down, my parents always loved me and gave me the freedom to be a free spirit. I had no idea what I was supposed to do, or what God wanted me to do, but I kept believing in Deuteronomy 31:6 (NIV): "Be strong and courageous. Do not be afraid or terrified because of them, for the LORD your God goes with you, he will never leave you nor forsake you."

Suddenly, doors began to open easily. My friend was a DJ for a local company in the area, and he needed someone to help excite the crowd at his weddings. They called the role a "motivational dancer" where my sole purpose was to go to events and encourage people to dance on the dance floor. What a fun job! Eventually, he began handing me the microphone and I graduated to an emcee where I would hype up the crowd and teach dances at a variety of events. I felt comfortable and at home doing this since I had always loved to sing and dance onstage. One day, I started playing around on his DJ controller. This was interesting, but I never imagined myself as a DJ. I had always thought about DJs as that old, weird guy at a kid's birthday party playing the "Cha Cha Slide." If this was God's calling for me, He must have quite a sense of humor.

Working at these events with the other DJs, I learned how to push all the buttons on the DJ controller, read the room, and mix the music with confidence. It felt easy and fun. I was definitely not the corny birthday DJ, but very much myself. In a weird way, it felt like all of my training in the theatre industry prepared me for this moment. God was speaking to me more and more to use the light inside of me. I fell in love with myself again, and felt proud of who I had become and who I was becoming. One day, my friend called to tell me his friend needed a female DJ in Orlando for a few events. Without hesitation, God told me to go. Not just temporarily, but to actually move. Fear had never been an obstacle in my life, and I felt prepared, so I trusted that He knew what was best for me. I obviously didn't have the best track record of trusting and leaning on my own understanding. Somehow I missed Proverbs 3:5 (NIV): "Trust in the Lord with all your heart and lean not on your own understanding."

So, on a whim and with God's support, I moved to Florida, knowing only two people in Orlando. I moved and the doors began to open more and more. I fell into opportunity after opportunity, which led me to the happiest place on earth: Walt Disney World. Little did I know that God wanted to use me on an even grander scale than I could have ever dreamed. I walked onto the stage at Hollywood Studios to headline as the DJ for the Star Wars fireworks, performing in front of thousands of people. This was way better than being a princess. I was given a microphone and a stage to spread joy through music and encourage the crowd to make memories that would last a lifetime. Finally, I knew God's purpose for me. Walt Disney World led to Carnival Cruise Line where I toured all over the world bringing others this very joy. And now, I'm back in my hometown running my own all female DJ entertainment company where I have built a team of encouraging and vibrant women ready to perform at any type of event. Our mission is to let our light shine before others, that they may see [our] good works and glorify [our] Father in Heaven (Matthew 5:16, NIV).

My windy, painful road led me to my purpose. I know now I am meant to bring others joy through music, creating lasting moments that people will cherish for the rest of their lives, and empowering other women to become the best they can be. Today, I get to make my own schedule (based on God's calling, now that I am actually listening), create events to inspire other female entrepreneurs and celebrate with others on the most important and magical days of their lives. These events also led me to my incredible husband, who is such a beautiful example of unconditional love. I am so grateful to God for showing me how to love myself first, so I could love my husband the way he deserves to be loved. Recently, my husband gave his life to Christ before our son was born, so he could be the best example for me and our newborn.

A new and better life for me truly began when I stopped believing the lies of the world.

I am living testimony that God's timing is always perfect. A new and better life for me truly began when I stopped believing the lies of the world. God created me to be who I am, perfectly imperfect. Jesus was perfect and people still hated him. So why do we weigh ourselves down with what others think of us? People will always have an opinion because their opinions are solely based on their perspectives. It's just a perspective; it isn't the truth. I learned recently that I need to stop trying to seek validation from anyone but Him. It's so hard when this world demands that we live by comparing ourselves to others. We must stop letting others dictate our future. When we ask permission from the world, we are visualizing a reality that is holding us back from our true potential, and these thoughts have so much power over us; they become our reality. One of the hardest lessons I had to learn was that I must choose love and forgive. I had to forgive those who persecuted me, used me, tried to label my identity with a virus, a sickness. I learned and now boldly claim that no one has that power over me except God. I praise [Him] because I am fearfully and wonderfully made. [His] works are wonderful, I know that full well (Psalm 139:14, NIV).

God gave us free will and the power to fulfill His destiny, but if we don't seek Him, we will wind up on the wrong road. It's a lonely road. One that I won't detour on again. They say if you want something, you have to say no to everything that stands in your way. It was time for me to say yes to the Lord so He could give me the desires of my heart (Psalm 37:4). God saved me. He physically lifted me out of the dust and placed me into the life I always wanted, the life my inner child and ancestors could only dream of.

Now I sit here looking down at my newborn son's perfectly crafted face, each feature developed in His timing, his bright eyes eager to understand and see the world for the first time. I understand now why He had me wait for this very moment to hold him and soak up these newborn snuggles. In this quiet, sacred moment, I see that every detour, every heartbreak, and every delay was shaping me into the daughter, wife, and mother God always wanted me to be.

The *Lemonade*

| I had to taste the sour lemon to appreciate
the one meant for my lemonade. |

In what areas of your life are you currently tying your self-worth to success, recognition, or validation from others—and what might it look like to root your identity in Him instead?

Can you think of a painful, humbling, or disappointing season in your life that may have actually been guiding you toward growth or purpose? What do you need to surrender or trust more fully to move forward?

"No discipline seems pleasant at the time, but painful. Later on, however, it produces a harvest of righteousness and peace for those who have been trained by it."
Hebrews 12:11 NIV

| Meet Melody Ganaway |

Melody is excited to become a published author this year. She received her Bachelor of Arts Degree in Musical Theatre Performance from Marymount Manhattan College in New York City.

She has had the honor of performing with Sesame Street Live, Walt Disney World, Carnival Cruise Line, Virginia Musical Theatre, and Busch Gardens. Melody is the proud owner of Melody & Company Entertainment, an all-female DJ entertainment company in the Hampton Roads area of Virginia.

She serves her community by creating events and retreats for women-owned businesses to network and learn how to manifest their dreams into reality.

Lemon-aide

the God who sees me

| Fran Grittinger |

*"We have this hope as an anchor for
the soul, firm and secure."*
Hebrews 6:19 NIV

Chapter 4

The God who sees me

Have you ever felt unseen or alone? There is a story in the Bible about a young girl named Hagar, a housemaid who served Abram and Sarai of the Old Testament. Through her circumstances of insensitive and unfair treatment, she felt despair and ultimately fled her master's home. Hagar's situation presented itself when God promised Abram and Sarai in their old age that they would have a son to continue their family line. Instead of waiting on His timing, Abram and Sarai took things into their own hands; Sarai gave Hagar to her husband and a son was conceived. Hagar was extremely upset about her situation and made a point of showing Sarai her dismay. In return Sarai started treating her maid harshly. Distressed and vulnerable, Hagar ran away and came upon a river-bank. She grieved her circumstances in deep sorrow and anguish. But God, in His great love and compassion, saw and comforted her.

> *"The angel of the Lord found Hagar near*
> *a spring in the desert; it was the spring that*
> *is beside the road to Shur."*
> *(Genesis 16:7, NIV)*

The angel told Hagar that God sees her in her distress.

Like Hagar, *El Roi*[29] is with me in my trials and distress. Knowing that God is always keeping careful watch over me fills me with comfort and joy. I have personally been seen by God in a hard season of my life. During a physical storm, I cried out to God and He answered. Just like Hagar, I was heard, seen, and comforted by God; I am *Fran-seen.*

Yes we can and should have joy through trials — our lemons in life.

"Consider it pure joy, my brothers and sisters, whenever you face trials of many kinds, because you know that the testing of your faith produces perseverance. Let perseverance finish its work so that you may be mature and complete, not lacking anything." (James 1:2–4, NIV)

I have joy because God sees me and He is with me! I can laugh and enjoy God's presence even through difficult circumstances. This is possible because I have trust and faith in God and know that He is a good Father. He allows hard things in my life for spiritual growth and dependence on Him. My joy overflows when He takes the ashes of those difficult circumstances and replaces them with a crown of beauty!

---

[29] *El Roi* is a Hebrew name for God meaning "the God who sees me."

"And provide for those who grieve in Zion—
to bestow on them a crown of beauty instead of ashes … "
(Isaiah 61:3, NIV)

A fresh start

I don't know about you, but I am thankful God gives us new mercies every morning.

"The steadfast love of the Lord never ceases; his mercies
never come to an end; they are new every morning … "
(Lamentations 3:22—23, ESV)

When we forgo our own desires and follow God's by listening to the promptings (those little nudges) of the Holy Spirit, joy will manifest in our lives.

I want to follow God's plan each day, but I usually miss the mark and go my own way. There is some solace in knowing we will never follow God perfectly, only Jesus did that. But we can start out our day with Him, reading scripture, praying, journaling, and resting in Him. Then, throughout the day, we can listen to the little nudges He gives us and say yes!

Each day is a "fresh" start. When we forgo our own desires and follow God's by listening to the promptings (those little nudges) of the Holy Spirit, joy will manifest in our lives. The Holy Spirit is in us the moment we have accepted Jesus Christ as our Lord and Savior. We are saved by grace through faith. One of the fruits of the Spirit is joy and we can live a joy-filled life every day—even through trials (our lemons)—when we partner with God and say yes to the things He has for us in obedience.

Yahweh, your way

For many of us, the word "obedience" can produce a sour taste in our mouths. It suggests we must leave our own wants and desires and submit to another's. The greatest act of perfect love and obedience in history was done by Jesus, son of God, when He submitted to His Father's will by courageously sacrificing His life on the cross and rising again on the third day to save all who believe. Jesus is our perfect example, and when we start to walk out obedience in our lives, we will produce sweet fruit.

He provides opportunities every day to say yes in obedience, and as we remain faithful, He entrusts us with more. Each opportunity we embrace deepens our relationship with Him, and through these experiences, His joy, peace, and love increase—and we want more! Just as an infant progresses through developmental stages—from drinking milk to eating cereal and solid foods, and from rolling over to crawling and taking first steps—our journey of obedience follows a similar pattern. God begins by assigning us smaller tasks and roles. When we say yes to them and join Him in His work, we prove ourselves faithful and demonstrate to God our readiness for greater challenges.

*"Whoever can be trusted with very
little can also be trusted with much."
(Luke 16:10, NIV)*

He stretches us and strengthens us, but He never leaves us on our own. He is always with us so we can have courage and know that whatever it is He has for us, it is all within His will and His timing. All of this obedience sanctifies our lives to look more and more like Jesus, expanding the kingdom of God, His great commission.

Living our lives out in obedience requires trust and surrender. I learned this truth in a personal way when God asked me to step into a boat during a field trip with my daughter.

Lemons to Lemon-*aide*

My youngest daughter's fifth-grade trip to a Christian camp was the start of a journey I did not want to be on—one so many other women have traveled and bravely fought. Breast cancer, an unwanted journey, was one of my many lemons, but *El Roi*, the God who sees me, came to my aid in a time of need. He is my "lemon-*aide*." In His great love and mercy, He blessed me with an unexpected messenger at the camp: another parent who helped me by sharing his wife's story of how she discovered that she had breast cancer.

I spotted this messenger in a group of parents that were there to help with the canoeing activity. I recognized him right away as someone I had gone to high school with years ago. I had never really talked to him back then, but he made me nervous nonetheless. I recall many of my high school memories as unhappy, and he was a reminder of that. Back then, I felt very self-conscious and struggled to fit in. I had been living my life comparing myself to other kids, which caused me great insecurity. Comparison left me feeling less than and never enough. So when I saw this messenger, all those insecurities came flooding back.[30]

I live in the same area where I grew up, so I often run into someone from the past and most often at the grocery store. Before I was recently delivered from comparison, if I would spot someone from that time in my life, I would usually dart to the next aisle—or better yet, to the other end of the store. At the camp, I wanted to dart and hide, but there were no grocery aisles to take refuge. I prayed, "Please God, don't put me in a canoe with him (my messenger), any other parent is fine!" But God in His infinite wisdom and sense of humor, orchestrated this dad and I to be assigned to the same canoe. I was nervous, annoyed, but amused all at the same time. I knew God had a sense of humor (just look at a picture of a proboscis monkey, and you'll know what I mean) and decided that His fun and perfect plan was getting me out of my comfort zone.

In the book of Matthew, Jesus' disciples were also out in a boat on a lake. They saw Jesus in the distance walking toward them on the water and were afraid. Peter desperately wanted to walk to Him and Jesus said "come." So Peter got out of the boat in faith and started to walk to Jesus. It wasn't clear to me at the time what God

---

[30] I wish I knew growing up and into adulthood that comparing myself to others is an imprisonment. It steals my joy and causes great pain and problems in my life. God did not create me or you to live out of comparison, and He even says it is foolish to do so (2 Corinthians 10:12, ESV). I learned recently that when I stop comparing myself to others, I can finally be myself! There is only one true me, uniquely and wonderfully made for a purpose planned before I was ever born! God says I am beautiful, and I am embracing that truth. We can fight and overcome comparison by reading God's Word, speaking it over ourselves, and believing deep within us that it is true.

"I praise you because I am fearfully and wonderfully made; your works are wonderful, I know that full well." (Psalm 139:14, NIV)

"For we are God's masterpiece. He has created us anew in Christ Jesus, so we can do the good things he planned for us long ago." (Ephesians 2:10, NLT)

was up to when He put me in that canoe. While Jesus asked Peter to get out of the boat, God asked me to get in.

Out on the lake, we watched kids in canoes grouped in pairs enjoying the day. I made the most of my situation by engaging in small talk and trying to think of things to say. We talked about our kids and other loved ones. I'm not sure how it happened, maybe he just needed to talk, but the conversation got real. He brought up his wife's breast cancer journey and the miracle of how she found out she had it. A friend of hers who had survived breast cancer stressed the importance of breast self-exams, explaining that she had discovered her own cancer that way. He went on to say that his wife did eventually listen to her friend, and after her own self-exam found something of concern. Through testing, it did turn out to be cancer.

After the canoeing activity was done, I said my goodbyes, thanked my new confidant for the special time talking, and said I would be praying for his wife. The next morning at home, after thinking about the unexpected conversation with this person from my past, I went ahead and did my own self-exam. I remember thinking at the time, *there's no way I'll find anything*. God wouldn't allow cancer, especially after I had just survived another life threatening medical issue, a pulmonary embolism (PE). That experience was terrifying, but it brought me closer to God. With a PE, I had no control if I would live or die; all I could do was pray, have others pray, and lean into my faith.

To my surprise and disbelief, I felt a small lump. *God are you kidding me right now?* I proceeded to schedule a mammogram. The resulting images did not show anything even though there was clearly a lump. After my PE experience, I learned the importance of advocating for my own health and wanted another opinion. I scheduled a second mammogram at another clinic. This scan revealed "something" in the area where I felt the lump, and so they scheduled me right away for a biopsy. I waited patiently for results for the better part of a week. They came back benign—no cancer!

Because I had a biopsy, the doctor told me I should have another mammogram in six months instead of waiting a whole year. At the six month mark, I went in again. The doctor noticed some changes in the images of this mammogram compared to the scan from six months earlier. It showed calcifications in the tissue. They did another biopsy and again, the waiting game. I received a call later in the week and listened to the nurse on the other end say, "I'm sorry, it is cancer but at a very low stage." She went on to say it was ductal carcinoma in situ (DCIS). Stunned in disbelief, I felt like a bystander hearing someone talk about someone else, but I knew she was talking to me about me. My eyes welled up and my voice was shaky; I could barely finish the conversation. There was some good news; it was found at a very early stage. After the phone call and some time to process, I had an overwhelming realization. Although I received a cancer diagnosis, I had also experienced a miracle!

Jesus, in His great love and mercy, put me in that canoe with someone who, by the grace of God, shared his wife's story and led me to my own early diagnosis. It is sobering to think what stage my cancer could have developed into had God not come to my aid. He is my lemon-*aide*.

After that unwelcome phone call, my cancer journey really began. I navigated so many doctor appointments and different specialists: doctors of oncology, plastic surgery, genetics, and more. There are so many hard decisions to be made with the various treatment options. It was all so much and overwhelming. After a visit with a genetics counselor, there was more unwelcome news; I had a variant of one of the breast cancer genes. At that time, they told me I had an 80 percent chance of reoccurrence and a 60 percent chance of ovarian cancer. My choices were either a lumpectomy with radiation or a mastectomy. I asked the surgeon what he would do if it was his wife or daughter. Based on my genetic results, he advised double mastectomies. Because I also had a high chance of ovarian cancer, he suggested getting my ovaries removed at the same time. The latter didn't bother me as much because I already had my kids, however, it would throw me into early menopause at age 44.

I listened to the doctor's advice. Once the hard decisions were made and my treatment plan was finalized, my first surgery (of five) was to happen before the end of the month. I recall breaking down one evening in bed and crying out to God. I remember there was a storm that night. I could see lightning flash through the skylight and hear the pounding of rain and the thunder roar. I cried loud-ly—a real, ugly cry—through the storm of my situation. But in the noise of the storm, something incredible happened: I heard an audible voice say, "You are beautiful." I knew instantly it was Jesus talking to me; I would never say that about myself. I felt a peace wash over me as He knew exactly what to say. *El Roi*, the God who sees me in my distress, had spoken. My *sour* thoughts sweetened and my storm calmed. I was in awe of my God and felt immense joy that He was with me and had turned my sadness into gladness.

About six months after my first surgery, around the time of my second one, I received a letter from my genetics counselor. This letter was a small bitter lemon within my larger breast cancer one. It stated that, after more study, my breast cancer variant was not at the high 80 percent risk of reoccurrence or 60 percent risk for ovar-ian cancer as they originally thought. My mind started to reel, and I could feel my face heat up with anger. *Would I have made the same decisions at the beginning to remove a part of myself and forever be phys-ically changed?* I was upset and angry. I knew it wasn't anyone's fault as I wanted it to be. I wanted to yell and scream at someone: the doctors, the genetics counselor, someone … I wanted to blame them for giving me wrong advice. As the bitterness was setting in, God revealed in my spirit that this was actually good news. It meant that my daughters, who could carry the variant, would not be at the high risk that I was at the beginning of this journey. I started to look at the situation in a new light. What's most important is that my daughters and future granddaughters would have a better outcome; more information should they need it to make good sound decisions. God took this bitter lemon and made it better! I have hope and look forward; what the enemy stole is only a temporary loss. God promises a new beautiful body in Heaven when He calls me home. I may not see it, but He sees me now as beautiful.

"The Lord does not look at the things people look at.
People look at the outward appearance,
but the Lord looks at the heart."
(1 Samuel 16:7, NIV)

He gave me a new, loving, and compassionate heart when I said yes to Jesus as my Lord and Savior, and I am forever grateful.

As I traveled this rough and winding road of "the cancer journey" I leaned into God more, and found that I could be a comfort and a good listener to other women in the same *boat*.

He recently reminded me at my fifth surgery, only a few months ago, what it is like to go through the whole process again: decisions, surgery, and recovery. It has been 10 years since I have had a surgery, and it's easy to forget all the pain, tears, and waiting to get back to regular life. I have a refreshed look at what other women have gone through and are going through today.

God is the only one who can take our pain and make a purpose. When I redirected my gaze from myself to Him, seeking His face and perspective, my burden lifted. I moved out of self-pity and moved into self-love, exchanging my ugly thoughts for what is lovely. With this renewed mindset, I love and serve others better and know God's peace, joy, and unending love.

Sweet joy

I'm only recently learning about laughing with Jesus. I hadn't realized until now how fun and fulfilling our relationship can be. I am getting to know His kind and gentle spirit more through journaling and can see His humor, too. I personally have a silly side and believe He has everything to do with that. He is not only my anchor in the waves and storms of life, but also my friend—and friends laugh together. I have found intimacy with Him as well. It is in my quiet time with Him when I seek His face and where our spirits join: There is joy, hope, and wonder. I see Jesus with me in a lovely field of bright, colorful wildflowers; hand in hand, laughing, dancing, and enjoying our time together. My love for Him grows in our quiet time together, and He leaves me wanting more of Him and less of the world.

Other times I find joy walking in nature and being in awe of every detail He designed, the beauty, colors, and sounds of creation.

I have great delight in my family; God blessed me with wonderful parents, a loving husband, and my three beautiful girls who add the sparkle to my life. There have been some growing pains throughout the years, but the sweet far outweighs the sour. And when the two blend together, it's a perfectly imperfect life with my loved ones. I have also experienced joy in the ministries He has called me to as well.

Prison ministry has been an unexpected blessing. Going into dark places and shining God's light to the lost, broken, and overlooked has created a deep seed of compassion and caring for others that God waters and continues to grow. I would always leave those prison walls more blessed than when I walked in, especially when witnessing women renew or give their lives to Christ.

A more recent ministry I am blessed to be a part of, Bloom Again, has brought abundant joy. God has connected me to a wonderful sisterhood in Christ. Not only is there joy in helping young girls and women at these gatherings find freedom from comparison so they can be themselves, but God in His great love has also multiplied friendships. There were so many wonderful moments at Bloom Again, but a few that stand out and warm my heart. At our second Bloom event, there was a beautiful flower crowning ceremony. Every woman and girl walked through a chuppah (a traditional Jewish wedding canopy) and was crowned a beloved daughter of the King. I was later told by a fellow Bloom leader, "Joy was pouring out of you at the crowning ceremony." And at the third and most recent Bloom event, my oldest daughter accepted Jesus Christ as her Lord and Savior!

How can we know the sweet without the sour?

I had to have the lemons to taste the lemonade; Jesus adds His living water and sweetness of joy to our sour, sometimes bitter lemons. He quenches our thirst for Him, then promises when we accept Him as our Lord and Savior, we will never thirst again. We become more like Him every day, and as we pour ourselves out serving others, the world sees Him. He doesn't cause lemons, such as cancer, to happen, but He allows trials to bring us closer to Him and mature our faith. He never promised a trouble free life, but He does promise to be with us through our hardships. Yes, we must have some lemons, but as a pastor once said, when we are squeezed, may Christ pour out![31]

---

[31] Nigel "Legin" Anderson, "When You Feel Like Giving Up" (sermon, Grace Bible Church, Virginia Beach, VA, November 2, 2025.

No matter our lemons, big or small, we will always taste God's goodness when we look past our momentary circumstances and look up to *El Roi*, the God who sees us!

I dedicate this chapter to my messenger—you know who you are. I also dedicate it to my husband Scott, who walked through this cancer journey with me and never made me feel less than, only beautiful (He also thinks the surgeons did a great job too, LOL!). Lastly, I dedicate this to my wonderful friend Kess, who always invites me and is the main reason I am a part of this cohort of authors.

A note from the author: Regular mammograms and breast self-exams are extremely important for early breast cancer detection. They can reveal changes, as they did for me, enabling timely diagnosis, less intensive treatment, and better lifesaving outcomes. These crucial exams support long-term health and offer reassurance through awareness and prevention. I urge you to take these critical steps to take care of yourself. I am still alive and well; a living testimony of the importance of early breast cancer detection.

The *Lemonade*

| Turning sour into *pour*fection! |

When you are squeezed by the trials and hardships of life, how do you recognize God's presence in the storm and allow Him to turn those sour moments into sweet peace and joy? How do you maintain these fruits of the Spirit?

What is a recent lemon situation you have gone through? Have you ever felt unseen like Hagar? Did that experience deepen your relationship with God or distance you from Him, and why?

"We have this hope as an anchor for the soul, firm and secure."
Hebrews 6:19 NIV

| Meet Fran Grittinger |

Fran is a mother of three beautiful girls and the wife of an amazing husband, Scott. She is also a breast cancer survivor, diagnosed in 2014. Through that journey, Fran began to pursue God's purpose for her life. In 2017, she was called into Prison Ministry and now serves as Treasurer of Kairos Outside of Eastern Wisconsin. Before Kairos, Fran volunteered with Prison Fellowship at Milwaukee Secure Detention Facility. Currently, Fran is CFO of SEEDS Ministry. She is also a table leader and speaker with Bloom Again, gatherings for women and girls to experience the love of Jesus. God is now calling Fran to build her own ministry, Beyond Compare, to help His daughters overcome comparison so they can live uniquely free.

Turning Lemon Blossoms into Blessings

Squeezed but Surrendered

| Kim Harrison |

*"And don't allow yourselves to be
weary in planting good seeds, for the
season of reaping the wonderful
harvest you've planted is coming!"*
Galatians 6:9 TPT

Chapter 5

Hi my name is Kim, and I am a perfumer, someone called and anointed to make perfume. I wrote this four years ago in "The Joyfull Entrepreneur."

God's timing and ways are perfect! As I write this, I'm in the process of the second launch. And by the time you read this, you will be able to smell the heavenly scents God called me to create. Proverbs 27:9 (ESV) says that oil and perfume make the heart glad and so does the sweetness of a friend's counsel that comes from the heart.

Guess what? I'm still in the second attempted launch of my perfume; I still believe Proverbs 27:9, and by the time you read this book, "Jesus Laughs," you should be able to smell and purchase the heavenly scents I created by the grace of God. This is a good place to laugh with me—and with Jesus—because back then I definitely thought that I would be a millionaire. I truly believed that once I created these fragrances—seven, to be exact—my business would be an instant success: famous (not in the sense of Hollywood fame, but perfume fame), married (beloved), and still living on the beach in Southern California (no explanation needed here). But God knew different.

"'For My thoughts are not your thoughts, nor are your ways My ways,' declares the Lord. 'For as the heavens are higher than the earth, so are My ways higher than your ways and My thoughts higher than your thoughts.'" (Isaiah 55:8–9, AMP)

So here we are now and I have decided to join my friend Tamra Andress and a host of other believers to share a bit of my story in the presence of Jesus—anchored in His joy, love, hope, and laughter. Even when we are called by God and walk in obedience to our assignment, it doesn't mean we know exactly how these things are going to be fulfilled or come to pass. In our itty-bitty minds—especially when compared to God—we somehow begin to think too small and want things too fast. The plans of God are enormous, and trusting that truth is the only way we can produce what we are being called to bring forth on earth. How else would we be able to depend on Him? I assure you—if you have a word from God, something He is requiring of you, lean in. We will not be able to excuse God out of the way with our own plans and ideas of how things should go.

Looking back over the last five years, I never for one minute thought it would be so much work. From the time God spoke to me about moving from New York to California with my son, making perfume for a specific person at a specific time, and stewarding the most beautiful projects, I could never have imagined any of it on my own. I had already prayed for an assignment for seven years. I had already said, "Yes, Lord, send me. Restore me." So why would God make me wait any longer? I moved to California in March 2021. God was with me. He fully provided for the journey ahead of me, and everything I left behind, I gave as a donation to others. I saw it as a blessing. It was during COVID, and I was starting fresh. I had the vision before my eyes. I had the verbal blessing from God. And yet, I was waiting. I didn't understand what I was waiting for. It seemed like every time I had done what God asked me to do, all of my circumstances remained the same. What changed was me. Each day I walked the beautiful beach shores of San Clemente and stood before the hilltop mountain views overlooking the sea. I was being transformed. You may or may not know that seeing is believing—and seeing shifts the atmosphere. Everything was new. The sights, the sounds, and the smells were things I hadn't experienced in a long time. Day after day, I was taken back to scents I hadn't smelled in years.

Jasmine and Natal Plum filled the air, romantically reminding me of the honeysuckle and tiger lilies that ran along the fence in the backyard where I grew up. The citrus groves in California were like nothing I had ever experienced in my life. The air was filled with blossoms I have never smelled before—oranges and lemons, to name a few. Months later, after smelling them far off in the distance, you would see the evidence of fruit hanging low on the branches—the evidence of a future harvest. This was my holy ground, a time for me and the Master to walk hand in hand. I learned so much about myself, people, life, and the undeniable favor of God. I learned how to see things from God's perspective. This was a season for Jesus to lead me and for the Holy Spirit to teach me. I learned so many things that even today it's hard to narrow down my testimony to one. What has been engraved on my heart and mind is this: God is good. God is love. And He will never leave us or forsake us.

While things didn't go the way I thought they would in California—some of it is still a mystery. What I do know is that God called me there for a time: to heal, to create, to refresh, and to experience my own personal revival. I know that one day He will call me back there. For the meantime, I'm in North Carolina, and it has been the battlefield of my life to date. But I have been trained well. My mind holds the smell of the beauty that unfolded before me. Those scents taught me to inhale, exhale, and breathe.

When God spoke to me, I thought all the things He spoke would happen immediately, but that was not the case. I think one of the most honest questions we can ask ourselves is this: How do we wait on God? What is our heart posture when it looks like nothing is happening? Will we still be obedient to God while living in the world? Is there still joy, laughter, and celebration? Do we still show up for people with a miracle mentality—ready to be used and to overflow?

I used to go on Instagram Live five days a week. The segment was called "Perfume and Prayer." One day the topic was laughter, which made me wonder: Did Jesus ever laugh? As I pondered it, I asked God to show me a passage where Jesus laughed or expressed joy. I was led to the wedding in Cana, found in John 2:1–11. Jesus was at a wedding celebrating with His disciples and His mother, Mary, was there as well. They feasted for many days, as was the custom, and the celebration was elaborate. Can you picture it in your mind? Can you imagine Jesus laughing and having a great time? Now let's look at the story.

> "Now on the third day, Jesus' mother went to a wedding feast in the Galilean village of Cana. Jesus and his disciples were all invited to the banquet, but with so many guests, they ran out of wine. And when Mary realized it, she came to Jesus and asked, 'They have no wine; can't you do something about it?' Jesus replied, 'My dear one, don't you understand that if I do this, it will change nothing for you, but it will change everything for me! My hour of unveiling my power has not yet come.' Mary then went to the servers and told them, 'Whatever Jesus tells

you, do it!' Nearby stood six stone water pots meant to be used for the Jewish washing rituals. Each one could hold about twenty gallons or more. Jesus came to the servers and instructed them, 'Fill the pots with water, right up to the very brim.' Then he said, 'Now fill your pitchers and take them to the master of ceremonies.' And when they poured out their pitchers for the master of ceremonies to sample, the water had become wine! When he tasted the water that had become wine, the master of ceremonies was impressed with its quality. (Although he didn't know where the wine had come from, only the servers knew.) He called the bridegroom over and said to him, 'Every host serves his best wine first, until everyone has had a cup or two, then he serves the cheaper wine. But you, my friend, you've reserved the most exquisite wine until now!' This miracle in Cana was the first of the many extraordinary miracles Jesus performed in Galilee that revealed his glory, and his disciples believed in him." (John 2:1–11, TPT)

While Jesus and His disciples were at the wedding, Mary told Him that the wine had run out. At first, Jesus responded as if the situation wasn't His concern, since He was waiting for His appointed time. But Mary, who had once said yes to the miracle of His birth, now trusted that His time had come.

This miracle wasn't just about providing more wine. It showed deeper truths about His servants faithfully obeying Jesus by filling the jars with water—even when they didn't fully understand why. In that moment, what seemed like an ordinary situation at a wedding became the setting for a miracle. What began with lack and embarrassment turned into abundance and laughter.

Moments have a way of shaping how we see life. Some are joy-filled celebrations we remember forever, while others are marked by sorrow and heaviness. I experienced one of those moments in a deeply personal way.

I lived in New York during 9/11, and there was so much sadness in the city. September 11 also happens to be my birthday. I was off from work that day, and I remember sitting on the couch crying for most of it. My mom insisted that I come out and at least have a little cake and ice cream. From that day on, I rarely celebrated my birthday—it just didn't feel the same. The tragedy of 9/11 had become a defining moment in our nation's history, marked by great sadness. My birthday felt stolen, which is no comparison to the many lives stolen that day. Whether you celebrate your birthday or not, it is undeniably the marker of the moment God ordained for you to enter the earth. So for almost 20 years, birthday after birthday felt uneventful. Yet God has a way of meeting us—even in the places where joy feels lost.

In 2014, I dedicated my life to Jesus, and the pruning began. Every branch that bears good fruit is pruned—cut back so that God can begin the growth process: the blooming, the emergence. "Every branch in Me that does not bear fruit, He takes away; and every branch that continues to bear fruit, He [repeatedly] prunes, so that it will bear more fruit [even richer and finer fruit]"

This is the waiting season—the season of waiting to see the mighty work of God. What will grow back? How much will grow back? What kind of harvest will be produced? This is all supernatural. We cannot see what is happening, but our spiritual fruits are being developed.

While that season of pruning was not easy, it was necessary. God was reshaping my perspective, healing places in my heart, and teaching me how to trust Him with every part of my life—even the places where joy once felt nonexistent. And in time, He began

We cannot see what is happening, but our spiritual fruits are being developed.

to show me that what felt stolen could be restored in ways I never expected—a party on the water.

God is so awesome. One of my testimonies has to do with my birthday, right before COVID. Though I had grown accustomed to not celebrating it, this year was going to be different. I had started preparing for my Jubilee year celebration. I was ready for God's best, and I was tired of not being present for my own birthday. God had given me a vision of a party on the water, so I began looking for venues. Early in 2020, COVID came, and the world was not the same as we had known it. There was no grand 50th birthday celebration that year as NY remained under strict restrictions. However, my sister graciously hosted a small, intimate gathering for me where she made Greek food because I love the Mediterranean lifestyle. Off and on I would think, *God showed me a party on the water.* Fast forward to September 10, 2021. I was living in San Clemente, a beach town, and my neighbor lived across the street facing the Pacific Ocean with the most gorgeous view. Knowing it was my birthday, my neighbor said, "I want to throw you a party. Just tell me who to invite, and I will do the rest." My friends Alex, Becca, some of my family, and new friends I had made came over to celebrate. We watched the sun set into the ocean, and the view was breathtaking. In a quiet moment I realized something: *I'm still 50 today* (because it was actually the day before my birthday). *I'm still in my Jubilee year, and I'm having a party on the ocean.* I started to cry. God really does want us to be happy, and He loves to hear our laughter. God did more than I could have ever imagined! That moment on the water was another reminder that God has always been guiding my story, even in seasons when I didn't recognize what He was doing.

Years earlier, I had written about my journey in another book called "The Joy-full Entrepreneur." In it, I shared how God slowly led me through decades of creativity as I worked with flowers, cosmetics, artistry, and design before He revealed my true assignment. What

I didn't understand at the time was that God was preparing me to work with fragrances all along, long before I understood my assignment. From the flowers in my childhood backyard to the Macy's Flower Show, the years of floral design and even my work in the beauty industry—all of it was training my senses for something I could not yet see.

Looking back now, I realize that my life has always been surrounded by fragrance. From the honeysuckle vines in my childhood backyard to the citrus blossoms I later smelled in California, God was teaching me something long before I understood it.

My home in San Clemente had lemon trees. Lemon blossoms became especially meaningful to me because they carry a sweet fragrance long before the fruit appears. The blossom is the promise; the fruit comes later. I was not only fascinated by the smell of blossoms in the air, but also by the harvest in people's backyards. Lemons fell off the trees daily and neighbors generously shared with each other.

At the time, in my waiting season, these experiences felt disconnected, but now I see that God was training my senses and creativity for something greater.

Waiting alone can be difficult because it can lead us to feel uncertain. We quickly learn that we are not in control, and the outcome can feel out of our hands. But when we make room for Jesus, He waits and works with us. Although we may be waiting, we can trust that our waiting is producing fruit—and the name of that fruit is patience (spiritually speaking). In the natural, it might even be considered lemons for the lemonade on the other side.

This is why it is so important to have Jesus in your life, God's love in your heart, and fellowship with the Holy Spirit. This is what I call the *perfumed life*—a life of abundance. It is the life Jesus has fulfilled for us through His birth, death, and Resurrection.

"A thief has only one thing in mind—he wants to steal, slaughter, and destroy. But I have come to give you everything in abundance, more than you expect—life in its fullness until you overflow" (John 10:10, TPT). This is the Word of God. This is Jesus speaking to us so we may understand that there is so much at stake when we wait with patience—it leads to a harvest.

Patience is like planting good seeds in the ground. We plow the field, we plant the seeds, we water the seeds, and then we wait. While we wait, God is perfecting us so that we become more like Jesus, who is the perfection of every gift of the Spirit. Patience is a beautiful fruit of the Spirit, and it is one of the fruits we must have in order to become mature believers.

"But the fruit produced by the Holy Spirit within you is divine love in all its varied expressions: joy that overflows, peace that subdues, patience that endures, kindness in action, a life full of virtue, faith that prevails, gentleness of heart, and strength of spirit. Never set the law above these qualities, for they are meant to be limitless" (Galatians 5:22–23, TPT). Did you hear that? Our fruits are meant to be limitless!

A practical way to wait with patience is through the combination of praise and laughter. Together, praise and laughter cultivate a spirit of joy and resilience, especially during seasons of waiting. When we celebrate through praise, we remind ourselves of the goodness and faithfulness of God, creating a focus that nurtures hope. Laughter, on the other hand, lightens our hearts and helps us not take our struggles too seriously.

By joyfully acknowledging what we are grateful for and finding moments of humor in our circumstances—our lemons in life—we develop a deeper sense of patience. This allows us to embrace the waiting period as a necessary part of our growth and journey, fostering contentment while anticipating what is to come. This kind of patient joy is much like the difference between a quick, convenient refreshment and something made with craft, care, and intention.

Now, imagine pouring a glass of store-bought lemonade sweetened with high-fructose corn syrup. It's quick, affordable, and intense, but the sweetness doesn't truly satisfy; it only leaves you wanting more. Now imagine making lemonade from scratch: patiently dissolving real sugar, zesting and juicing fresh lemons, then mixing it all with water to create something balanced and refreshing. In the same way, when we wait and allow God to work through our circumstances, He squeezes the best from life's lemons, adds a sweetness only He can provide, and finishes it with what truly satisfies—His living water. Though I didn't always understand what God was doing while leading me from the hilltops and lemon blossoms of California to where I am now in North Carolina, I've learned to wait well and trust Him to turn my lemons into the most satisfying lemonade.

The *Lemonade*

| I was used to instant lemonade—but Jesus prefers the kind made from real fruit. |

Can you identify a "lemon blossom" moment in your life—an early sign or promise from God that has not yet fully come to fruition? What might God be teaching you in the waiting season between the blossom and the fruit?

In what ways might God be developing patience, faith, or spiritual fruit in your life right now? How can you remain hopeful and joyful while waiting for His promises to unfold?

"And don't allow yourselves to be weary in planting good seeds, for the season of reaping the wonderful harvest you've planted is coming!"
Galatians 6:9 TPT

| Kim Harrison |

As the visionary founder of Flower Heart Perfumes, Kim Harrison has woven together three decades of experience in the beauty and fragrance industry, with time spent at prestigious brands like Clinique, Chanel, MAC, Jo Malone, and Bobbi Brown. These experiences shaped her path to become a trendsetting perfumer, a role that aligns with her God-given destiny.

Her beauty background is complemented by her studies at the Parsons School of Design, where she mastered the art of floral arrangement. Each bloom she arranged spoke volumes, just as each fragrance she creates does. Now, Kim has answered a calling by developing a line of perfumes imbued with passion, personality, and inspired significance. Each fragrance is crafted to awaken the senses and invite a deeper connection to the divine. Kim invites you to experience the transformative power of Flower Heart Perfumes and discover how scent can enrich your journey through life and spirit.

The Sour Shock

How Jesus Turned my worst day into Holy wonder

| Rachel Kemp Schoen-Kiewert |

"The Lord your God is with you, the Mighty Warrior who saves. He will take great delight in you; in His love He will no longer rebuke you, but will rejoice over you with singing."
Zephaniah 3:17 NIV

Chapter 6

What shattered my life became the very place where Jesus taught me how to breathe again—and somehow, how to laugh.

There are sentences that you never think you will say out loud. "I found my husband dead," is one of them. Even now, it catches my breath and sends pain to my heart. The words feel foreign, like they belong to someone else's story—but they are mine. That moment split my life into before and after. There was the woman I was when I woke up that morning—and the woman who went to bed later that night knowing nothing would ever be the same.

Shock was a strange sort of mercy from God, a kind of holy numbness. Decisions were made. Calls were placed. I asked others to help with food and household duties. People filled my home. I moved through it but reality had not set in. I was still waiting for my husband to come home from work or for his usual phone call when he left the parking lot. My body knew something catastrophic had happened, but my heart had not yet caught up.

Then the numbness wore off and the pain set in. It wasn't dramatic or loud. It was suffocating. It was the realization that I would wake up every day for the rest of my life without him. It was the weight of explaining our forever angel to our children. It was the sudden understanding that the future we had planned together had dissolved in an instant.

Breathing became work. I don't mean emotionally. I mean physically. I remember sitting in my kitchen one morning, maybe a week or two later, and feeling like the air could not go into my lungs. The shock had left. Grief had wrapped itself around my chest. I immediately started worshipping with my 2-year-old. That's all I could do.

And then I realized I could not do this on my own; this was the hardest thing I had ever done. I turned to God and said, "You are going to have to breathe for me." Not metaphorically. Literally. I needed Him to be my oxygen. I needed him to be my nervous system. I needed Him to be the strength in my legs and the clarity in my mind. I had children who still needed breakfast. A 2-year-old who still needed to be picked up. A home that still needed a mother.

Psalm 34:18 (NIV) says, "The Lord is close to the brokenhearted and saves those who are crushed in spirit."

I had read that verse before, but I had never needed it to be more true than this present moment. And I found out quickly that He was who I needed to cling to—not my husband's friends, his family (who were not even speaking to me), or even my own friends who were trying to help. My God was going to be my lifeline. I grew closer to Him than I ever imagined.

My God was going to be my lifeline. In those weeks that followed, my house became a sanctuary. Not because it was peaceful, but because I worshipped in every room. I worshipped in my kitchen with tears running down my face. I worshipped in my living room with my 2-year-old spinning in circles beside me. I worshipped in my bedroom at night when the silence felt unbearable.

And somehow, in the middle of the most traumatic season of my life, something remarkable began to happen. God did not just sustain me. He began surprising me. Instead of only giving me strength to endure, He began pouring love into places that felt hollow. Joy would rise up in moments where sorrow should have swallowed me whole. Laughter would bubble out—unexpectedly, perhaps even inappropriate by some standards—but undeniably real. At first, I questioned it. I thought, *Is this okay? Am I allowed to feel this?* As I watched my 2-year-old laugh with glee every day, I said, "I wanna be like her. I can be like her. I can laugh, smile, and relax my nervous system."

But the more I leaned into Him, the more I realized something profound: Jesus was not offended by my laughter. He wanted me to feel joy alongside the heaviness. He was participating in it with me.

Nehemiah 8:10 (NIV) says, "The joy of the Lord is your strength."

I used to think that meant joy comes after strength. I learned that sometimes joy itself is the strength. There were days when I felt joy and I felt lighter. I was less exhausted and I could float through the day—and yet somewhere inside me would rise up and crack a joke. I would say something lighthearted about "playing the dead husband card," and people would look at me unsure whether to laugh or correct me.

> But the more I leaned into Him, the more I realized something profound: Jesus was not offended by my laughter.

But I knew. Jesus was laughing with me. Not at my pain. Not minimizing it. But defying it. It felt almost rebellious—this holy humor in the face of devastation. It was as if Heaven was whispering, "This does not get the final word."

My youngest child was two at the time. Two-year-olds do not live in yesterday or tomorrow. They live in the present. She woke up with delight in her eyes. She danced in the kitchen. She was pure joy and laughed from her belly. She climbed into my arms as if nothing in the world was broken.

I began to notice something divine. Children have such a clear path to the Holy Spirit. They haven't spent years layering fear, logic, and guardedness over their faith. They simply feel love without questioning it. They receive joy without analyzing it. Watching her, I realized something: God was preaching to me through my child.

Zephaniah 3:17 (NIV) says, "The Lord your God is with you, the Mighty Warrior who saves. He will take great delight in you; in His love He will no longer rebuke you, but will rejoice over you with singing."

I had never pictured God singing over me. But in those days, I began to sense it. In the kitchen. In the quiet. In the middle of tears, there would be this gentle awareness—like a hug you cannot see but can feel.

Later, a few women from church gathered around me and walked me through inner healing. They taught me something that changed everything: how to receive a "God hug." When my mind drifted back to the traumatic images—the ones that try to replay when grief surfaces—I learned to pause and invite Jesus into the memory. To envision Him there. Not as a distant observer, but as the God He is: present, compassionate, protective.

And when I did, something shifted. Instead of being trapped in the worst moment of my life, I could feel His arms around me. I could sense Him steadying me. I could feel warmth where there had been ice. I now have a new relationship with God.

Though it did not erase what happened, it redeemed how I carried it. It is possible to feel sad and smile in the same breath. It is possible to grieve and receive joy.

For weeks, I relied on God to help
me breathe. But slowly, He began
teaching me how to live again.
Not in denial. Not pretending.
But with a new awareness that life is fragile, holy, and far too precious to postpone joy. I realized that this happened so I could live
life differently.

Then came another shock. Another moment that took my breath away—but this time for a different reason. In the aftermath of unimaginable loss, I discovered I was carrying a bundle of joy. I was pregnant.

The biggest joy bomb I could experience with my two children—who were thrilled to have a baby join our family—erupted when I shared the news with them. My oldest started jumping up and down and pumping his fists like he had won the World Series. This moment confirmed God has amazing plans for me and my children.

It was as if Heaven said, "Here. This baby will heal your heart. These children will give you even more purpose. This child will carry joy into places that feel impossibly heavy—into grief-soaked mornings, into questions without answers, into the future you weren't sure you were strong enough to face." My heart overflowed in prayer: *Thank you God, thank you for being by my side, holding me up when I couldn't do it myself, helping me love my children and live our new life.*

Isaiah 61:3 (NIV) speaks of God giving "a crown of beauty instead of ashes, the oil of joy instead of mourning."

I had read that verse in seasons that required mild encouragement. Now it was blazing on the pages of my life. Ashes and oil. Mourning and joy. Sorrow and laughter. All coexisting.

My oldest son had been in Florida with family when my husband passed. He stayed there a little longer, protecting him from the immediate shock. When he returned home, he was devastated. But he was also strong in a way that startled me. He would tell me, "Mom, I feel him right here." He would put his hand over his heart and say, "Papi is with us."

Children sense what adults debate. He wasn't quoting theology, he was expressing intimacy. And in his childlike confidence, I found strength. I realized that my children were not only ones I had to be strong for—they were vessels of strength for me.

Our home did not become free of grief. But it did become full of presence. God's presence and Jesus' laughter. Though our home experienced its greatest loss, my children and I discovered a new relationship with God. We talked about Heaven. We talked about love. We talked about how God's plans are bigger than what we can see. And slowly, my perception of life shifted.

I no longer saw time as something to manage. I saw it as something to cherish.

I no longer assumed control. I surrendered.

The sour shock—the moment that shattered everything—became the bold differentiator in my life. It forced me into radical dependence. It stripped away superficial faith and left me with something raw and real.

I learned that I could not water down my trust in God anymore. I needed Him as my breath.

For laughter. For parenting. For sleep. For purpose. And He met me. Right where I was with His arms wide open, with love. Not with timelines. But with tenderness.

I have received so many blessings since my husband passed that sometimes it is hard to dwell in the trauma. That does not mean I do not miss him. I miss him in moments big and small. I miss him in laughter and in silence. If you knew my husband, you knew he did everything with great passion. I miss his passion and energy with the kids. I miss his immense love that he showed us all. But I know God has a plan and I trust in the Lord more than I ever have.

The initial sour shock became the very place where awe was born. And sometimes, when I crack a joke that makes others uncomfortable, I feel it again, that holy companionship with my God. I see God's fingerprints everywhere—in my children, in my community, in the baby God gifted me even when I thought my heart could not hold another layer of emotion. In the unexpected joy that would arise at the most inconvenient times.

Jesus did not simply comfort me—He transformed me. And He didn't stop at transforming me. I now know that He sings over me. He took what was sour beyond comprehension and turned it into something that makes people pause and wonder. How can she laugh? How can she worship? How can she speak of joy?

Because I met a God who hugs. A God who breathes life into lungs that feel collapsed.

A God who rejoices over His daughters. A God who is not intimidated by tragedy.

And a Savior who, in the middle of my tears, smiled and said, "I'm still writing this story."

The *Lemonade*

| The day my world shattered, Jesus laughed. So I laughed back and thanked Him for the blessings that keep on coming. |

What has been your sour shock? Is there a moment that split your life into before and after? Take a moment to name it and ask the Lord to fill your heart full of love.

When you think about your most painful memory, can you picture Jesus present with you? What changes when you imagine Him standing beside you and embracing you with a God-sized hug?

"The Lord your God is with you, the Mighty Warrior who saves. He will take great delight in you; in HIs love He will no longer rebuke you, but will rejoice over you with the singing."
Zephaniah 3:17 NIV

| Meet Rachel Kemp Schoen-Kiewert |

Rachel Kemp Schoen-Kiewert is a faith-led wellness entrepreneur, chief creative chick, and devoted mother of three—Giovanni (9), Iliana (2.5), and Mateo (just 3 weeks old when she wrote this chapter).

After the devastating loss of her husband, Freddy, Rachel chose to rebuild her life anchored in Christ, determined to create a legacy of joy for her children and herself. With a deep passion for restorative health and natural living, she helps others steward their mind, body, and soul while balancing their hormones and losing weight.

Rachel believes her God-given purpose is to help others live a blissful life—not because life is easy, but because joy is possible even in the deepest pain. Through faith, resilience, and natural products, she continues to find strength in the Lord and to build a new life rooted in purpose, healing, and hope.

A Bittersweet Summer

The Squeezed Season

| Cara Pinder |

"These troubles and sufferings of ours are, after all, quite small and won't last very long. Yet this short time of distress will result in God's richest blessing upon us forever and ever."
2 Corinthians 4:17 TLB

Chapter 7

I had a 2-year-old son living at my parents' house 300 miles away, while I lay in a hospital bed. This wasn't how I envisioned my final months of pregnancy. As the saying goes, "If you want to make God laugh, tell him your plans!" This is not because He is spiteful, but because His plans are sweeter than our expectations.

"'For I know the plans I have for you,' declares the Lord,
'plans to prosper you and not to harm you,
plans to give you hope and a future.'"
(Jeremiah 29:11, NIV)

Everet wasn't easy to bring into the world; he was a 5-pound baby who was breech and scheduled to be born by c-section. This isn't unheard of in most countries, and everything went as scheduled. He became the joy of my existence.

After his delivery, they discovered my heart-shaped uterus and a few other complications would make it difficult for him to have a sibling. Our wonderful doctor informed us she couldn't specify how many children I could have, but one more would likely be the maximum.

A little over two years after Everet was born, I was expecting baby number two! While visiting my parents, my husband, Jerry, and I took our son for an ATV ride around the homestead. When we arrived back at the house, I used the bathroom and saw there was blood. For a moment, I forgot I was pregnant and thought I had gotten my period. After I came to my senses, I realized I needed to get to the hospital.

We waited in the ER. They ran some tests and told me I couldn't ATV anymore because it was probably too aggressive on my uterus. I chuckled and told them we couldn't have gone any slower, as we had our 2-year-old with us, and we were taking a leisurely tour. They told me to be careful and sent me on my way.

A week later, we were back home. At 2 a.m, I had to pee. Blood again—more this time. Back to the ER we went. We walked in, and I told them I was feeling fine and that this had happened before. They strapped all the monitors they could find to me and did some tests. After what felt like hours, they informed me that I didn't just lose some blood but that I was also losing amniotic fluid. More time went by, then the doctor came back into the room to inform me I would be having this baby as soon as I was flown to a bigger hospital. I wasn't even seven months pregnant, and in disbelief. I tried to wrap my head around the situation and requested we drive in the morning. Instead, I was told I needed to be flown immediately—I would need to be strapped down to be medically evacuated to and from the plane. I informed them I could walk just fine.

Strapped onto a plank with nurses on all sides, I took a discomfited 45-minute flight. I had no change of clothes or overnight bag and was now more than 100 miles from home. Rolled into a room on another plank, I met my nurses and doctor in my pajamas and slippers. Tests were done, and they were hopeful that I had not lost too much fluid. The doctor said he was going to do everything he could to keep my baby safe inside my belly for the foreseeable future because the lungs were not fully developed. I signed papers giving them permission to give me a high dose of steroids to expedite lung development, just in case my baby needed to be delivered soon.

With my unborn child's life in the forefront of my mind, I agreed. Shortly after I took the steroids, there were side effects. I started puking, followed by a migraine that made me want to tear my skull from my body. They couldn't get it to break, so I was given a sedative and surrendered to a deep sleep.

I peeled my eyes open, completely unaware that a day and a half had passed and I was still lying in a hospital bed. It felt like a terrible hangover. The doctor arrived back at my room and told me he was optimistic about keeping the baby in my womb as long as possible since we made it through the first 48 hours. I had never felt more disoriented.

I was told I would be staying there until my baby was born. I was not allowed to leave my bed except for quick bathroom breaks after the catheter was removed, or for nurse-assisted baths—no showers. Each night, I slept with leg compressions, and tests were run every three hours. I could go for a 15-minute wheelchair cruise with a nurse once a day, but my main goal was to stay flat and grow my baby.

I wanted to be sitting by the water and sipping lemonade, not ordering off a generic hospital dinner menu day after day.

I lived in that hospital for five weeks. My son went to live with my parents while my husband worked. We were all hours away from each other. My emotions were high. Summer was my favorite season, and I was watching mine coast by while I lay there. It felt like my own prison. I was mad. I wanted to be with my son and husband, not monitored every three hours like a science project. I wanted to be basking in the warm weather, even if I was largely pregnant and a bit swollen. I wanted to be sitting by the water and sipping lemonade, not ordering off a generic hospital dinner menu day after day.

I was mad at God. I hated when people came to visit me because I didn't know the outcome of all of this, and I felt I had to put on a positive face.

I broke down and cried hard. Through my tears, I started to pray, but my heart was still full of anger as I spoke to God. I was praying because I was afraid—my least favorite reason to pray. I wanted my prayers to come from gratitude, but in that moment, I was more uncertain than ever. With no delivery date in place, I just lay there, day after day.

Later that week, my parents came to visit and brought me a package. Inside was a small lap quilt, made with many different scraps, and a note. It read:

> Just a note to go along with this prayer quilt. You are being prayed for. Each stitch represents the prayers being said for you. A quilt tells "God's story."
>
> The top has many pieces, like our lives; some are dark, and some are colorful, like our walk through this world. My seams don't always match up on my quilts, which reminds me that our road is not always straight. The warm filling in the middle is the Holy Spirit, warming our souls and encouraging us. The back of the quilt is one piece, and He is the One and Only God. The ties are what bind us together with His unconditional love. God can take all of the pieces of our lives and create a beautiful pattern and blanket us in love. I hope you can wrap this around you, not only for warmth, but to feel His love and presence. Love, Allie

I hadn't seen Allie for years, but I knew this was more than a quilt. When I was 10 years old, she was a helper at our church youth group. I went up to her and asked if she would help me ask Jesus to be my Savior. We prayed in the old pews that day, and now, years later, she was sending me not only a quilt, but also a reminder of God's love.

It was at that moment that I decided if this was where my life had led me, I would do my best with my time in the hospital. There was a craft cart at the hospital for patients, so I utilized that. It was pretty picked over, but I started making paintings for the nursery. I asked my mom to bring a quilt we had been working on so I could bind the edges while I lay there. I started watching "American Ninja Warrior" in the evenings, which boosted my spirits. Then I started anticipating my family's visits. People called, prayed for me, and came to see me. This all helped those warm summer days move a little faster inside that third-floor window.

It was early August when they set a date: I would deliver this baby on August 7. I had signed a lot of papers while in the hospital, but the days prior to the surgery were extensive. I had to sign papers allowing them to do all sorts of things, one of which was consent to give me a hysterectomy in the case of an emergency. They were anticipating the delivery to be difficult (no sugar coating there), so I consented to a PICC line, which is a larger IV line typically used for chemotherapy.

The day was finally here. I barely slept the night before, knowing a tough road was ahead. They rolled me into the operating room and prepared me for an epidural. I'd had one before, and my pain tolerance was strong, but this time was different. I started to shake—uncontrollably. I was good at calming myself down and breathing through tough situations, but I couldn't catch my breath. They proceeded with the needle as if I were at the DMV and there was a line. At first, they asked if I was cold, and I shook my head no. They treated me with kindness and tried to calm me. I continued to shake, my whole body knew. They started acting annoyed, saying they couldn't insert the needle unless I stayed completely still. My double-IV hands gripped my knees as I bent forward. They managed to proceed, and I became like a talking head in a glass jar. My arms lay straight out by my sides, and a blue sheet draped across me like they were going to perform a puppet show.

Everything started off normal. There seemed to be an adequate number of people in the room and lots of chatter on the other side of the blue curtain. Jerry sat next to me. We had never spent this much time apart since we met, and now we were at a loss for words. He was optimistic and shared positive reinforcement with me like, "You got this, babe!"

I started to get tired, really tired. Jerry kept up the small talk, trying to keep me awake. He'd say, "We have to meet this baby, just stay awake a little longer!" I dozed in and out. I heard the doctor ask for more people. Nurses flooded the room, which felt like a stampede of horses. I heard the doctor say the baby was stuck under my ribs due to being breech, a twisted umbilical cord, and my heart-shaped uterus. They began to cut me more deeply, and in a sheer ripping moment, I started to feel everything.

I started to scream at my husband, telling him that I could feel everything. It was a mere whisper to the world, but my brain was screaming. I moaned again that I could feel everything. The anesthesiologist agreed I was running out of time on the epidural and asked the doctor how he wanted to proceed. "I just need more time, just a little more time," the doctor yelled. My mind heard them bicker like two people trying to detonate a bomb. Moments passed, and then we heard, "The baby is out!" The doctor hoisted up the child in a Simba-like hold, and my husband praised, "It's a girl!"

They placed our daughter, Fallan, by my face for just a moment and relieved us with the news that she was breathing. When they took her over to get cleaned up, something quickly changed, and she was no longer breathing. I heard the nurses say they needed to get the baby to the NICU right away. In the same few moments, the doctor yelled that I was losing too much blood. I saw my husband's face turn white as he looked frozen in time, torn between two life-threatening moments. A slew of nurses started holding my legs straight up in the air, and I could see my toes above the curtain. The pain and pressure were severe, and I heard him say, "Put her under. We are losing time." I wanted to know what was happening with my baby girl, but my eyelids were like cinder blocks. My eyes shut, and I realized I was dying.

I woke up like it was all a dream, still in a hospital bed. I started to move, and it hit me, excruciating pain. I lifted the sheet, and every part of me was bloated; there were staples keeping my insides in and yellow stains from the antiseptic. Jerry came into view, and he asked if I wanted to meet our baby girl. A huge dark cloud covered my body and mind, and I replied, "No." I turned my head away and drifted back to sleep. Almost two days passed, and when I woke, Jerry and the nurses encouraged me to go see my baby. Weak from surgery and having not walked in five weeks, I was wheeled through the slender halls of the NICU in my bed.

There she was. Tiny. The room was silent. Lying in a clear incubator, she lay there with a feeding tube in her nose and monitors attached everywhere. I was only allowed to touch her through a gloved hole in the side of the tank, and it felt like a scene in a sci-fi film. At that moment, I felt useless.

I was wheeled back to my room, where there was discussion about the four blood transfusions and two iron transfusions given to keep me alive. No hysterectomy was performed, but instead an old-fashioned technique of packing my uterus. My doctor, who was nearing retirement, said this may have saved my life. The downfall was that there was a football field length of cotton clotting my uterus, which would have to be removed before I left the hospital. I almost thought he was joking, but when I glanced at the nurse beside him, I realized he was not.

On day 4, I was finally able to spend some time with Fallan. I felt such guilt, such disconnect. We didn't get that first breath of life skin-to-skin moment, and I barely wanted to meet her at first. I was so depleted and so ashamed of how I felt. Because of my recovery and her weighing only 5 pounds, she was immediately fed through a tube. She lived in an incubator for the next 10 days, and I tried desperately to nurse her every three hours, but I also had to supplement with purchased breast milk. I felt like a failure. My husband did everything he could and stayed by our baby's side when I couldn't. I prayed that things would get better for all of us. I knew we had to keep moving forward.

Days went by, and I was no superstar at nursing, but we kept it up and had lots of skin-to-skin time when she wasn't in her little incubator.

I was beyond grateful we were both alive, but it shook my faith. On one hand, I had seen prayer and human kindness in action, and I had a beautiful, new baby girl. On the other hand, I wondered why this was my path. At this point, I knew the recovery would be a long road, and I felt lost on how I would manage to take care of a baby and a toddler while healing.

> *On one hand, I had seen prayer and human kindness in action, and I had a beautiful, new baby girl. On the other hand, I wondered why this was my path.*

August was nearly over before Fallan was breathing on her own and starting to gain weight. Two more weeks had passed, and it was my birthday when they finally released us to go home.

As we walked up to our front door as a family of four, we were greeted by balloons and gifts covering the porch. I glanced over at my husband, holding our baby girl, then down at my son clinging to my leg. In that moment, I felt the love of God, family, and friendship.

I spent the following year in physical therapy while our family kept a low profile, closely watching our newborn who struggled with respiratory issues and influenza. Early on, a nurse reassured me that one day it would all feel like a distant memory. At the time, it sounded like bedside manner, but more than a decade later, I can now see that she was right. Everyone is healthy and thriving. Watching my children grow with curiosity inspired my writing career; their endless questions ultimately led me to become a children's book author.

By God's grace, we are given this life, and now we bask in summers filled with warm sunshine and sweet lemonade.

The *Lemonade*

| By God's grace, we're gifted life—and summers of sunshine and sweet lemonade. |

Think back to a time when life handed you lemons and there was no sugar in sight. How did that season shape you, and in what ways did it make you stronger?

Have you ever experienced a bittersweet season when life felt sour and God seemed quiet? What brought you comfort and helped you keep your faith?

"These troubles and sufferings of ours are, after all, quite small and won't last very long. Yet this short time of distress will result in God's richest blessing upon us forever and ever."
2 Corinthians 4:17 TLB

| Meet Cara Pinder |

Cara Pinder is a Montana writer whose favorite people call her "Mom." After writing for years, with zero intention of releasing it publicly, Cara's children inspired her to share her talent and passion with the world.

"The Tooth Fairy's Stars," the first publication in its series, launched her career and uplifted her commitment to writing. Cara insists we let children be little, not grow up too fast, and have faith in things greater than what we can simply see.

When Cara isn't writing or doing laundry, she revels in the precious time she gets to spend with her family in this fast-paced world. Cara feels most free while fishing on the lake in the warm sun or adventuring down a snowy mountain on a snowboard. Find out more at CaraPinder.com.

A Sweet Celebration

Where the sour becomes song

| Kimberly Price |

"Those who plant in tears will harvest with shouts of joy."
Psalm 126:5 NLT

Chapter 8

By August of 2019, life had taken on a sourness I could no longer ignore. I had been chasing clarity with everything I had—programs, coaches, certifications—any path the world promised would lead me back to myself. But the harder I tried to outrun the restlessness inside me, the heavier it all felt. Each new attempt left me more hollow than the last, hinting that the real fracture was deeper than anything I could fix on my own. I didn't know it then, but the unraveling had already begun, and even in the ache, God was quietly clearing space for a sweetness I had long forgotten.

Physically, I looked fine. Strong, even. But the world doesn't give medals for surviving what it doesn't understand. People move on. Life moves forward. And I was left standing in the quiet aftermath of my own story, changed, aching, and unsure what to do with the pieces of myself that no longer fit.

My children were growing older, stepping into their own identities while I slowly slipped away from mine. Their independence revealed a truth I had been avoiding: I no longer knew who I was if I wasn't needed every moment of the day. The roles I had clung to so tightly—mother, helper, achiever, survivor—were beginning to fall away, and with them went the scaffolds I had built to hold up my worth.

Friendships suddenly felt shallow. Social spaces felt loud. Even the good things—the courses, classes, and coaching containers I believed might "fix" me—seemed to magnify the ache. Shame stacked upon shame in tall, wobbly layers I could barely carry.

And yet, even in the heaviness, I never truly disconnected from Jesus. Somewhere in the fog, I kept praying, journaling, and studying Scripture. My spirit clung to the thin edge of hope like a thread woven through the fabric of every breath. A faint flicker glowed deep inside, the kind of holy spark that refuses to be extinguished even when everything else feels dark.

Trauma doesn't ask permission. It rises slowly, like a tide you don't notice until the water is suddenly up to your chin. Years of pain, loss, striving, and survival had been stacking inside me, and the weight began pressing upward. My masks were impeccable. People saw confidence, strength, resilience. But behind the scenes, I was running on emotional fumes and spiritual muscle memory.

Life felt fragile. My identity felt fractured. Not because of one moment, but because years of carrying too much had finally caught up with me. I didn't need to relive every detail to know the truth: I was exhausted from holding everything together. And God was beginning to show me that He had never asked me to.

By that point, there wasn't one defining moment that led to the invisible wall. It was the slow, quiet accumulation of years of striving, searching, and realizing that the life I had built no longer aligned with the inner stirring I was beginning to feel but didn't yet understand.

> *Trauma doesn't ask permission. It rises slowly, like a tide you don't notice until the water is suddenly up to your chin.*

I had always been a hard worker, an achiever, a visionary with big dreams and even bigger expectations for what my life might become. When I was diagnosed with Stage IV cancer in 2009 at 34, I believed I had been given a second chance—not just to live, but to do something meaningful with my life. I imagined there were still years ahead of me to become the woman I felt stirring deep in my soul, to build something significant, to make a difference that mattered.

Before I knew it, a decade had passed, and I was 44. Somewhere along the way, the dream I carried for so long began to feel like it was slipping through my fingers. According to the world's standards, I hadn't made the "big, bold impact" I thought my life was supposed to hold. Instead, it looked like I had been jumping from one thing to another trying to find the path that would finally make everything make sense.

Inside, I was drowning under the weight of what hadn't worked. Regret began surfacing: old traumas, poor decisions, moments I wished I could rewrite. Lies started whispering louder and louder:

You should have done more by now.
You've wasted your second chance.
You're running out of time.
You've let everyone down.
You're not who you thought you were.

By late summer, it felt like I was losing my grip. Ten years had passed since my diagnosis, and instead of feeling established or fulfilled, I felt like I was treading water in a life that no longer made sense. I had run out of excuses, and the hardest truth of all was the one staring back at me: I felt like I had let everyone down—but most of all, myself. All the dreams I once carried so confidently now felt like fragile echoes. I reached the kind of exhaustion that settles into the bones, the kind that whispers lies about your worth and your future.

I'll never forget the night I hit that invisible wall. The house was quiet, the kind of quiet that feels heavy instead of peaceful. The soft glow of the hallway light spilled across the floor as the rest of the house slept, and I lay there, staring into the dark, tears tracing familiar paths across my face. I felt empty in a way I had never known before.

And in that moment, the only name that felt safe on my lips was Jesus.

Again and again, through trembling breath: **Jesus … Jesus … Jesus …**

And for the first time in a long time, I stopped trying to fix my life and simply let Him meet me there. In that moment, Scripture was truer than I knew: "The Lord is close to the brokenhearted and saves those who are crushed in spirit" (Psalm 34:18, NIV).

I don't remember the dream I had that night, but I remember the morning, because something was different. Not dramatic. Not cinematic. Just … lighter. As if hope had quietly slipped through the cracks while I slept.

It felt like the fulfillment of a promise I didn't yet understand: "Weeping may endure for a night, but joy comes in the morning" (Psalm 30:5, NKJV).

A whisper rose in my spirit:
Stop running. Stop striving. Stop reaching for worldly answers. Come home.

So I did the only thing that made sense: I canceled everything. Every program, every coach, every plan I had signed up for out of desperation. I didn't "arrive" that day. But the shift had begun. A crack of light had made its way through the wall around my heart.

Later that year, the Lord gave me a single word for the season ahead: **surrender.**

And Scripture stood before me like a doorway: "Trust in the Lord with all your heart and lean not on your own understanding; in all your ways submit to Him, and He will make your paths straight" (Proverbs 3:5–6, NIV).

Looking back now, I see that surrender wasn't the end of something; it was the beginning. The beginning of truth shaking loose the lies. The beginning of identity rising through the rubble. The beginning of hope finding her voice again. The beginning of Jesus teaching me, step by step, how to dance with the sour.

> *Dancing with the sour didn't mean the past suddenly tasted sweet.*

Dancing with the sour didn't mean the past suddenly tasted sweet. It meant learning how to move through the memories without being swallowed by them. It was the strange, sacred place where pain and healing coexist, the way a mother remembers the agony of childbirth but holds the memory through the joy of the life it brought forth. The pain was real, but it no longer had the power to define the story. Jesus began teaching me how to hold the past differently. Not denying it, not pretending it didn't hurt, but letting Him transform it into something that could grow me instead of break me.

Little by little, He showed me that the sour parts of my life were no longer my prison; they had become my teacher. They were the places where my strength had been forged, where my faith had deepened, where my identity had been quietly rebuilt. What once tasted bitter began to carry the unexpected flavor of grace. The memories were still there, but they no longer owned me. I could look at them the way you look at a scar, with evidence of a wound that once existed, but also proof that healing had taken place. That was the dance. Not erasing the sour, but learning to move with it in a way that revealed God's redemption inside it.

If I could whisper to the woman I once was, the one curled up in the dark whispering His name, I would tell her: *You are not alone. You are not forgotten. Your story is not over.*

And I would remind her of the identity she didn't yet know was hers: "Fear not, for I have redeemed you; I have called you by name; You are Mine" (Isaiah 43:1, NKJV).

But I didn't know any of that yet. I was still in the sour. Still learning the sound of His footsteps drawing near. The dance, the one I never knew my soul was made for, was only just beginning.

The Squeeze

The squeeze was the unmaking, the holy pressure God allowed not to break me, but to reveal what had been buried for years. As I look back through my journals, I now see what I couldn't see then: I had been seeking God all along, but without knowing how to include Him in the depths of my daily life. My prayers were sincere, but my understanding was shallow; my heart loved Him, but it didn't yet know Him.

Before the unraveling, there were whispers. Small fissures in the facade I had worn for decades. Moments when the smile didn't quite fit, when the striving didn't soothe, when the noise inside me grew louder than the truth. Something deep within was awakening, a quiet knowing that the life I was living was far too small for the soul God created in me.

There were days I stood in a room full of people and felt a canyon inside my chest. A distance between who I was and who I was pretending to be. It was like standing at the edge of a bridge I didn't know how to cross. I could sense both worlds, the one collapsing and the one calling. It wasn't dramatic. It was holy erosion. A gentle undoing recognized only in hindsight.

When the squeeze intensified, it didn't feel spiritual, it felt like loss. Like confusion. Like God had pulled me into a desert without a roadmap. Only later did I understand: **the wilderness isn't punishment, it's preparation.**

This became the season of excavation. God began uncovering what I had buried: lies about my worth, pressure to perform, the hurt I carried for others, the trauma I disassociated from, and the shame that masqueraded as humility. I had carried so much that wasn't mine, so others wouldn't have to feel it. In doing so, I silenced myself.

God did not rush the unearthing. He is too gentle for that. Instead, He revealed each layer slowly, through songs, walks, Scripture, unexpected tenderness, and long nights of honesty. Healing felt like being taken apart. Truth felt like being rebuilt. Every time an old identity surfaced—the victim, the achiever, the fixer, the invisible one—God whispered a new one. Slowly … the wilderness became a sanctuary.

Over time, every season of squeezing brings the soul to a point where it cannot stay the same. For me, there wasn't a single revelation; it was a series of holy interruptions. For me, that moment wasn't a single revelation; it was a series of holy interruptions. Most of them came after surrender, after I finally quieted myself long enough to hear Him and then chose to respond. Looking back, every surrender was met with doubt, and every act of obedience carried resistance. The steps God asked of me were rarely dramatic, but they were almost always just outside the borders of what felt comfortable. And yet, every time I said yes, even with trembling faith, He met me there.

There comes a moment in every season of squeezing where the soul realizes it cannot stay the same.

Sometimes He met me in the pages of my journal, where thoughts I didn't know I was thinking would pour out like answers waiting to be discovered. I remember one morning sitting with my pen hovering over the page, unsure what to write, when a single sentence came pouring out faster than I could process it: *Are you willing to let go of what you think you know, for what I want you to know?* I sat there staring at the words, realizing they were as much instruction as they were comfort.

Other times He spoke through Scripture, a verse suddenly rising off the page as if it had been written for that exact moment. There were days when His voice arrived through the wisdom of a friend, the quiet encouragement of family, or the unexpected clarity that came while walking alone in nature, moments where the world seemed to pause just long enough for my heart to recognize His presence.

At the time, the pieces rarely made sense. Each step felt small, sometimes confusing, and often slower than I wanted. Just when I thought I understood what God was doing, another interruption would come, another moment where His truth gently corrected mine. What I thought was forward, He would turn sideways. What I thought was the answer, He would unravel. Over and over again, my understanding had to be turned right side up by the beautiful upside-down nature of His kingdom.

But looking back now, I see what I could not see then: He was guiding every step. Every surrender laid another stone in the foundation He was building. Every act of obedience expanded my trust. Every interruption was an invitation to know Him more deeply.

God rewired me with truth one surrendered inch at a time. He showed me that obedience is a doorway to deeper knowing, forgiveness is freedom, feeling isn't weakness, healing requires surrender, identity cannot be manufactured, and sanctification is not punishment but promise.

The lies fell off like scales, not all at once, but one blinding layer at a time. Breakthroughs came disguised as ordinary days. Conviction sliced through decades of self-protection. And in the midst of reconstruction, God whispered, "**I have always been preparing you**."

The wilderness had not been wasted. The pain had not been pointless. The pressure had not been punishment. It was all formation, a reordering of my heart, mind, and identity, and woven through it was a quiet Scripture that guided me forward: "In all your ways acknowledge Him, and He shall direct your paths" (Proverbs 3:6, NKJV).

Before the sweetness of celebration arrives, there is often a hint, a quiet moment when the light shifts and you realize you're not who you once were. Joy began showing up in places I never would have expected. I had spent years racing through life at 90 miles an hour, believing happiness would be found in the next accomplishment, the next milestone, the next place I could go or thing I could achieve. But somewhere along the way, God began teaching my heart to recognize a different kind of joy.

It appeared quietly, almost unexpectedly, in a sunrise that stopped me in my tracks, in a breath of fresh morning air that suddenly felt like a gift instead of a routine. It showed up in the laughter of my children echoing through the house, in the warmth of a simple hug, in the fleeting glance of love from my husband across the room. Moments I once rushed past began to glow with meaning.

Gratitude started rising in places I had overlooked for years: the miracle of waking up, the rhythm of my breath, the sacredness of ordinary moments. I wasn't chasing joy anymore. I was discovering it had been surrounding me all along. Slowly, I began seeing my life through His lens instead of my own.

Peace settled where fear once lived. Forgiveness began to feel like freedom. Scripture came alive. My heart started recognizing the Lord's voice, not as a distant echo, but as a familiar presence.

I didn't yet know the fullness of what God was doing, but I could feel the veil thinning, the bridge appearing, the pieces aligning.

The squeeze was not the end.
It was the doorway to celebration.

Sweet Celebration

There is a moment in every sanctifying journey when the pressure eases, the veil thins, and the soul realizes it has stepped into something entirely new.

Becoming didn't arrive with a trumpet blast; it arrived with recognition—the quiet but undeniable awareness that the God who had undone me, pressed me, refined me, and rewired me was now revealing me. Not the me I had built or protected or performed into existence, but the me He created before the world began to bruise me. This is the miracle of sanctification: You wake up one day and realize you are no longer living from your wounds; you are living from His wholeness. As that realization settled over me, it felt as if Heaven itself widened around my life.

Then, in a way I can only describe as holy, weighty, unmistakable—the Lord Himself seemed to reach into my life and pull back every mask I didn't know I was wearing. Suddenly nothing was cloudy anymore. Nothing was tangled. Nothing was out of reach. For the first time, I could see why the undoing had been necessary, why the pressing had been sacred, and why the delays were not denials but developments. Every break had been preparing me for blessing. Every rejection had been a redirect. Every unanswered prayer had been protection.

I heard these words settle into the deepest part of me: "Therefore humble yourselves under the mighty hand of God, that He may exalt you in due time" (1 Peter 5:6, NKJV).

Due time had arrived, not because I earned it, but because God decided the chrysalis had done its holy work.

People often imagine elevation as God lifting us higher, but elevation actually begins when God makes us empty enough for Him to raise us His way. I had to lose the identities that were never mine, let go of the habits that numbed me, surrender the lies that shaped me, and stop clutching the life I had built so I could receive the life He designed. Only when my hands were finally open could He place purpose in them, and only when my heart was finally quiet could He speak identity into it.

In that stillness, He said, "Daughter, this is who you are."

Not what life told me. Not what pain convinced me. Not what failure whispered to me, but who He says I am: chosen, anointed, set free, redeemed, loved, called, prepared … a warrior who carries His fire.

Years earlier, long before I understood what sanctification would require, God had given me a vision: women rising, healing, becoming, standing in their identity with boldness and beauty. The dream flickered during my cancer diagnosis and dimmed in seasons when I felt unworthy. But God's visions do not die, they wait. And as He rebuilt me, He resurrected the call He had placed on my life: BE.

Be whole. Be restored. Be renewed. Be rooted. Be everything He spoke over you before the world ever tried to name you. The becoming was never just for me. It was for the women who will rise because I did. My testimony has become their invitation.

The celebration itself did not arrive as a single moment; it unfolded as the unveiling of an entire life. One afternoon, sitting alone in my office after years of revelations, I looked around at ALL that surrounded me: journals, books, vision boards, prayers, pictures, dreams, and scribbled ideas that had followed me through every season. And now, for the first time, I could see it clearly—every single thread of my life represented in some small way and uniquely woven together by God's hands. The provision. The preparation. The protection. The promises.

And I laughed.

Not the polite kind of laughter, but the kind that spills out when Heaven suddenly makes sense. I laughed with Jesus the way a daughter laughs with her father when she finally understands the story he has been writing all along.

> *Not the polite kind of laughter, but the kind that spills out when Heaven suddenly makes sense.*

Somewhere along the way I realized something unexpected: Jesus hadn't just walked me through the sour, He had been teaching me the steps all along. What once felt like survival had quietly become a dance. The sorrow was still part of the story, but it no longer led the rhythm; now, grace did.

Butterflies can be found throughout my office, and in that moment, the image felt unmistakable. The caterpillar never understands the chrysalis while it's dissolving, but the butterfly sees the whole sky waiting. I had spent years in the wilderness wondering what God was doing, but in that quiet moment, I realized He had been preparing me to fly.

The sour had become a song.
And the dance had only just begun.

Sister, if He did it for me, He will do it for you. The undoing is not the end. The pressing is not your punishment. The wilderness is not abandonment. The waiting is not wasted. The struggle is not failure.

It is sanctification. It is preparation. It is becoming.

You are being shaped into the woman God already sees. And there will come a moment when you look around your own life and realize the sour didn't break you and the squeeze didn't crush you, it prepared you for the sweet.

You will emerge. You will rise. You will become. You will celebrate. Because Jesus does not just save. He restores. He renews. He transforms. And yes sister, He celebrates!

You were pressed, not to perish, but to pour.

"Those who sow in tears shall reap in joy."
(Psalm 126:5, NKJV)

And one day you will realize, the very thing that almost broke you, became the place where God taught you how to dance.

The *Lemonade*

| You were pressed, not to perish, but to pour. |

Where in your life is God not punishing you but preparing you, and what part of your story might turn sweet if you surrendered it to Him?

Where in your own story has the sour been preparing you for a sweetness you haven't yet seen, and what would shift if you dared to believe that God is already at work beneath the surface?

"Those who plant in tears will harvest with shouts of joy."
Psalm 126:5 NLT

| Meet Kimberly Price |

Kimberly Price is a holistic health practitioner, functional nutrition coach, speaker, podcaster and founder of BE, a movement devoted to helping women reconnect with who they were created to be—whole in spirit, grounded in truth, and fully alive in their identity. Through her work, Kimberly creates trusted spaces where women are invited to step out of performance, pressure, and survival mode, and into healing, clarity, and becoming.

A Stage IV cancer thriver, Kimberly's personal journey through illness, healing, and deep spiritual transformation reshaped not only her life, but the way she walks alongside others. What began as survival became surrender—and ultimately, a calling to help women rediscover their strength, worth, and God-given identity.

At the core of everything she builds—from programs and retreats to conversations and community—is a simple mission: to inspire and empower women to step out of survival and be who they were created to be. Kimberly believes that even the hardest seasons can become a testimony of strength, purpose, and celebration.

She lives this message not only in her work, but in her life—as a wife and mother of 4 incredible kids, continually learning, surrendering, and growing alongside her family.

Pressed for Zest

When Crushing met the Laughter of Jesus

| TashaRenèe |

"For I,' declares the Lord, 'will be a wall of fire around her [protecting her from enemies], and I will be the glory in her midst.'"
Zechariah 2:5 AMP

<h1 style="text-align:center">Chapter 9</h1>

A Testimony of Redemption, Restoration, and Holy Triumph

There are moments in a life that do not merely occur, they are ordained.
Moments that do not simply arrive on a calendar, but descend from eternity like sacred appointments written in invisible ink long before the heart understands their meaning.
There was a time I believed redemption was a distant word,
a promise written for stories that did not resemble mine.
But Heaven had already written my name inside mercy.
Before I ever knew the sound of my own healing, Heaven sounded the echo of my restoration.
Before I ever lifted my head in confidence, Heaven had already crowned my identity.
Before I ever stood whole,
Heaven had already declared me redeemed.
Redemption is not a cosmetic change.
It is not a motivational phrase.
It is not a surface adjustment or a polite correction.
Redemption is Resurrection.
It is the divine act of taking what was fractured and breathing life back into it
until the broken pieces no longer define the picture but are pieced together to become a prophetic mosaic—a masterpiece.
Restoration is not simply getting back what was lost.
It is receiving what was always intended.
True holy triumph is not the absence of my scars.
It is the presence of Yahweh's glory because of them.

Triumph is walking into rooms where your past once whispered
and realizing it no longer has a voice.
Triumph is standing where shame once shouted and hearing only
the laughter of Jesus instead.
There is a holy audacity that comes with being redeemed —
a sacred boldness that rises when you realize that what tried to end
you
has now become evidence that God sustained you.
This is not a story about surviving alone.
This is a story about being seen by Heaven when you feel invisible
on earth.
This is not a narrative of human strength.
This is the unfolding of divine mercy.
Because redemption does not merely change behavior, it trans-
forms your identity.
It does not simply silence the past,
it reincarnates destiny.
There comes a moment when you understand that Grace was never
chasing you to condemn you.
Grace was chasing you to claim you.
And when that realization settles into your spirit, something shifts.
You stop running from your testimony
and start walking in your authority.
You stop apologizing for your scars
and start recognizing them as sacred signatures of survival.
You stop whispering your story
and begin declaring it with reverence.
For every daughter who has ever wondered if redemption could
reach her, this testimony stands as living evidence:
Mercy does not expire.
Grace does not grow weary.
Love does not miscalculate.
And when Heaven restores,
it does not restore halfway.
It restores wholly.

Mercy does not expire.
Grace does not grow weary.

This chapter is not merely recollection,
it is revelation.
It is the unveiling of what happens
when Divine Love interrupts human history.
Because there are encounters that do more than inspire you.
They redefine you.
There are moments that do more than comfort you.
They commission you.
And there are seasons where Heaven steps into the timeline of your life
and rewrites what the enemy believed was permanent.
This is one of those moments.
This is the testimony of a life
not merely repaired, but resurrected.
A story not merely retold,
but redeemed.
A journey not merely survived,
but sanctified.
And before the first memory surfaces,
before the first tear forms,
before the first revelation unfolds—
know this:
The laughter of Jesus was already echoing before the pain ever began.
Because redemption was never an afterthought.
It was always God's plan.

November 5th was not simply an invitation.
It was a predestined appointment—a holy ambush of mercy, arranged long before my feet ever touched that ship, long before I understood the language of destiny, long before I realized Heaven had been tracking me through every chapter of my life.
It was not a coincidence.
It was a convergence.
A divine intersection where time bowed to eternity,

and memory bowed to mercy.
This moment was not accidental.
It was built in the unseen.
Planned in the courts of Heaven.
Scheduled in the scrolls of destiny.
Heaven had already written the moment.
The coordinates were set.
The atmosphere prepared.
The wind instructed.
The room assigned.
The memory scheduled.
The healing ready.
The laughter of Jesus already echoing in the unseen.
And I—unknowingly—was walking into a holy collision with redemption.
When my sister Deb Fasone invited me to An Evening Under the Son, I thought I was saying yes to an event.
A gathering.
A dinner.
A night out.
A social moment.
What I did not know was that I was stepping into a divine rehearsal of resurrection—a sacred encounter where the Light Himself would escort me back through a chapter I believed had long been closed, folded, and archived far from memory.
But Jesus does not forget what He redeems.
He revisits it—
not to shame,
but to showcase His victory.
He returns not with accusation,
but with affection.
He does not reopen wounds—
He reveals healing.
He does not drag the past forward—
He reframes it in glory.

The Drive—When the Past Began to Breathe Again
As we drove, the roads began to feel familiar.
The curves of the streets whispered stories.
The rhythm of the turns felt like echoes from another life.
The smell of the air carried a quiet nostalgia—as if memory itself
was traveling with me.
Even the lighting felt reminiscent,
as though the atmosphere recognized me
before I recognized it.
And suddenly, my spirit recognized something
before my mind could form language for it.
Memories stirred.
Not invited.
Not summoned.
Not rehearsed.
Not requested.
They rose like incense from a hidden altar—
from places I did not realize still held breath.
Moments.
Scenes.
Emotions.
Echoes of a woman I used to be.
A version of me buried beneath years of healing.
Beneath leadership.
Beneath ministry.
Beneath becoming.
Beneath surviving.
Beneath overcoming.
A woman I once was—
not erased,
but redeemed.
I didn't ask for them.
I didn't want them.
Yet Abba allowed them.
Not to wound me.

Not to shame me.
Not to drag me backward.
But to love me forward.
Because sometimes the Father allows the past to brush against the present—
not as a chain,
but as a contrast.
So you can see
how deeply,
how thoroughly,
how beautifully
you have been redeemed.
And in the quiet sanctuary of my spirit,
I heard Him whisper:
"Daughter … look at where I found you."
Not with disappointment.
Not with accusation.
Not with disgust.
But with tender awe.
As if He were saying:
"Look at how far My grace has carried you."
"Look at what My blood has rewritten."
"Look at the miracle you have become."
And I felt the holy paradox—
grief and gratitude,
sorrow and celebration,
reverence and relief swirling together like sacred incense.

The Ship—The Place Where My Past Once Spoke Loudest
The last time I remembered stepping onto the Spirit of Norfolk,
I was not the woman I am today.
Back then, I was an exotic dancer
performing for applause that never healed me.
Dancing for affirmation that never satisfied me.

Stripping for attention that never filled the hollow chambers of my soul.
I was a mistress.
Entangled in counterfeit connections.
Feeding wounds disguised as love.
Chasing validation in rooms where destiny could not breathe.
I lived in shadows.
I lived in numbness.
I lived in fragments, broken pieces of identity trying to survive in systems that profited from my pain.
I thought I was lost.
But Heaven knew I was chosen.
I thought I was hidden.
But Heaven knew I was marked.
I thought I was discarded.
But Heaven knew I was destined.
And this is where Jesus laughs.
He laughs at every lie that said I was finished.
He laughs at every verdict that said I was ruined.
He laughs at every whisper that said I could never become more.
Because while I was trying to survive,
He was already scripting my redemption.
While I was trying to cope,
He was already preparing my calling.
While I was trying to numb pain,
He was already guarding purpose.
While I was trying to disappear,
He was already preparing my visibility in glory.

This Time—Heaven Held the Pen
This time, the narrative was not written by trauma.
This time, the script was not shaped by wounds.
This time, the storyline was not dictated by shame.
This time, Heaven held the pen.
This time, the scroll read Redemption.

This time, I boarded not as a woman seeking validation—
but as a Redeemed Daughter.
Whole.
Called.
Crowned.
Clothed in dignity and honor.
Not because life had been easy—
but because His grace had been faithful.
This time, I did not step onto that ship to entertain.
I stepped onto it to encounter the Lover of my soul.
This time, I did not come searching for approval.
I came standing in identity.
This time, I did not arrive with regret.
I arrived with revelation.
And the atmosphere could feel it.
Heaven could feel it.
Hell could feel it.
My spirit could feel it.
A daughter had returned …
not broken, but crowned.

Psalm 23—The Banquet in the Presence of Every Lie
There truly was a table prepared
in the presence of my enemies.
Not people—
but spirits.
The enemies of shame.
The enemies of rejection.
The enemies of depression.
The enemies of abandonment.
The enemies of lies.
The enemies of feeling unloved, unwanted, unseen, and not
enough.
And there I was—
sitting.

breaking bread.
laughing.
belonging.
beloved.
Not as a woman searching for love in all the wrong places,
but as a woman deeply, eternally, irrevocably loved by LOVE Himself.
Jesus had not only restored me—
He had hosted me.
He had not only healed me—
He had honored me.
He had not only forgiven me—
He had feasted with me.
And I could almost hear Him laughing,
not mockingly, but triumphantly.
Laughing at the enemy's failed plans.
Laughing at every trap that did not work.
Laughing at every attempt to destroy what God had preserved.

Kavod on My Steps—Calvary in My Breath
This time, I stepped onto that ship
not with shame in my story,
but with the *kavod*[32] of Yahweh's glory resting on my life.
My steps carried the sound of Calvary.
My posture carried the evidence of resurrection.
My presence carried the testimony of a woman rewritten by blood.
Every step whispered:
"She survived what was meant to kill her."
"She carries oil from brokenness."
"She is proof that redemption is real."
"She is evidence that Jesus saves."
Transformation looks like this:

---

[32] *Kavod* is a Hebrew word that means "glory," with the root meaning of weight, honor, or significance. See Strong's H3519.

You can revisit old places
and not recognize the woman you used to be.
You can stand in familiar spaces
and realize the chains that once held you
no longer exist.
You can look at yesterday's pain
and see today's purpose.
You can look at old scars
and laugh—
because Jesus healed what the enemy hoped would haunt you.

The Rollercoaster—Breathless, Holy, and Alive
Redemption is not linear.
It loops.
It climbs.
It plunges.
It spins.
It jolts.
It steals your breath.
It awakens your tears.
It surprises your expectations.
And this night felt like a holy rollercoaster—
the kind you wait hours in line for,
anticipating every rise and fall,
every twist and drop.
There were moments I wanted to weep.
Moments I wanted to shout.
Moments I wanted to worship.
Moments I wanted to laugh—
that deep, belly laughter
that only comes when you realize:
"I should not be here … but GRACE brought me anyway."
And somewhere in the dips,
the turns,
the trembling pauses—

I realized:
Jesus has been laughing this entire time.
Laughing not because pain is funny,
but because pain did not win.
Laughing not because wounds were small,
but because His victory was bigger.
Laughing in the messy middle
because He already knew the
ending.
He laughs at Hell's agenda.
He laughs at the enemy's strate-
gies.
He laughs at every verdict spoken over my life.
Not arrogantly —
but victoriously.
Laughing because what the enemy meant for destruction
became a platform for displaying His glory.
Laughing because Hell wrote an obituary
and Heaven wrote a sacred invitation.
Laughing because the girl who once hid
behind shame, rejection, and abandonment
has become the woman who hosts His Presence.
Because He had already written

Psalm 23 over my story:
A table prepared.
A cup overflowing.
Oil poured freely.
Goodness and mercy pursuing relentlessly.
A banquet where pain once planned my funeral.
And He laughs because the feast is real.
He laughs because I am still standing.
He laughs because I am still called.
He laughs because I am still chosen.
He laughs because I am still loved.

My Testimony—My Life Redeemed as Daughter
Beloved, the last time I stepped onto the Spirit of Norfolk,
I was broken.
But this time …
I came whole.
Redeemed.
Restored.
Rewritten by Love Himself.
This is not theory.
This is not theology.
This is not poetry alone.
This is my life.
My testimony.
My evidence.
My miracle.
This is what happens when Abba steps into a story:
He turns shame into testimony.
He turns darkness into destiny.
He turns pain into purpose.
He turns a past into a platform.
He turns wounds into worship.
He turns mourning into laughter.
And somewhere in the middle of it all—
between tears and triumph,
between scars and songs—
Jesus laughs.
He laughs at what did not destroy me.
He laughs at what did not defeat me.
He laughs at what did not break me.
He laughs because He knows my end from my beginning.
And now when I look back,
I do not feel shame—
I feel gratitude.
Because the same Jesus who found me in the shadows
now sits with me at the table.

And He is still laughing.
Laughing with joy.
Laughing with triumph.
Laughing because redemption always gets the final word.

To the Reader—Jesus Laughs Over You, Too

If you are reading this
and remembering your own past …
If you feel the ache of former chapters …
If you wonder whether grace can rewrite you …
Let this testimony remind you:
Jesus laughs at what tried to destroy you.
Jesus laughs at every failed plan of darkness.
Jesus laughs because your story is not over.
Jesus laughs because redemption is louder than regret.
And He is laughing hysterically—
not at you,
but for you.
Because He already saw your ending
before your beginning ever unfolded.
Because He already wrote your restoration
before your breaking ever happened.
Because He already prepared your table while the enemy was still
planning your downfall.
And when you finally see it—
when you finally stand in the fullness of who He redeemed you to
be—
you will laugh, too.
Not in denial.
Not in disbelief.
But in holy triumph.
Laughing because what tried to destroy you
could not.

Laughing because what tried to silence you
failed.
Laughing because your testimony
is proof
that Jesus laughs.
And if your heart trembles while reading this …
If your breath catches in your chest …
If memories try to whisper louder than hope …
Hear this—not as poetry,
not as inspiration,
but as truth sealed in Heaven's courts:
Hell will never have the last laugh over you.
Not over your life.
Not over your name.
Not over your destiny.
Not over your children.
Not over your calling.
Not over your past mistakes.
Not over your hidden tears.
Not over your silent prayers.
Not over the nights you thought no one saw you breaking.
Not over the mornings you rose anyway.
The enemy may have had a moment,
but he will never have the final word.
Because the One who laughs last
is the One who reigns forever.
There is an ancient confidence that rises when you realize
that redemption is not fragile—
it is Resurrection power.
This is not optimism.
This is not denial.
This is not pretending pain never happened.
This is standing in the holy assurance that pain does not author
destiny—Christ does.
There is a Scripture that echoes this truth with thunder:

"The Lord laughs at him [the wicked one—the one who oppresses
the righteous],
for He sees that his day [of defeat] is coming"
(Psalm 37:13, AMP).
He laughs—not because evil is amusing,
but because evil is temporary.
He laughs because darkness has an expiration date.
He laughs because shame has an ending.
He laughs because lies collapse under truth.
He laughs because what tried to destroy you
does not outlive the promises spoken over you.
And when Heaven laughs,
it is not cruelty—
it is certainty.
It is the laughter of a King
who already knows the outcome of the battle.
It is the laughter of a Savior
who already walked out of the grave.
It is the laughter of a Father
who already prepared a table while enemies were still plotting.
So when you feel surrounded,
remember—
you are also covered.
When you feel delayed,
remember—
you are also destined.
When you feel pressed,
remember—
you are also preserved.
Because the same laughter that echoed over my redemption
echoes over yours.
The enemy may have tried to write a conclusion,
but Christ wrote a continuation.
The enemy may have tried to close the book,
but Christ wrote another chapter.

The enemy may have tried to bury the story,
but Christ resurrected the author.
And somewhere in the unseen realms,
above the accusations,
above the regrets,
above the what-ifs and the if-onlys—
Jesus laughs.
He laughs because your name is still written in mercy.
He laughs because your future is still drenched in promise.
He laughs because grace is still louder than guilt.
He laughs because redemption is still stronger than regret.
No shame will have the last word.
No failure will have the last word.
No betrayal will have the last word.
No addiction, no label, no diagnosis, no abandonment, no rejection …
none of it gets the final say.
The final say is Christ.
And Christ is laughing!
Not in mockery of your pain,
but in triumph over broken chains.
This laughter is not dismissive.
It is definitive.
It is Heaven declaring:
"You've overcome what was meant to silence you."
"You rose from the ashes where others expected you to remain."
"You became what darkness said you never could."
And when the day comes that you stand fully in the light of who
you were always meant to be,
you will not only remember the pain,
you will remember the laughter that outlived it.
You will laugh through tears.
You will laugh through gratitude.
You will laugh because you will finally see that Grace was working
even when you were weeping.
Because the enemy never had authority—

Only noise.
Only delay.
Only illusion.
But Jesus is the final Word.
Jesus is the final Victory.
Jesus is the final Laugh.
And His laugh, Beloved, is the sound of redemption echoing into eternity.

The *Lemonade*

| Redemption has the last word ...
and it sounds like Jesus laughing. |

If my scars are sacred signatures of survival, why do I treat them as disqualifications rather than evidence of mercy and grace?

What would it look like to stop living inside the chapter that wounded me and begin writing the legacy that will outlive me?

"For I,' declares the Lord, 'will be a wall of fire around her [protecting her from enemies], and I will be the glory in her midst.'"
Zechariah 2:5 AMP

| Meet TashaRenèe |

TashaRenèe, D.Min. (Hon.) is a prophetic evangelist, teacher, transformational spiritual wellness coach, and three-time published author with more than 25 years of ministry leadership. She is the visionary behind SacredSecretsRetreat™, a sacred gathering created to restore and strengthen women in leadership through prophetic teaching, inner healing, and spiritual formation.

Known for her poetic prophetic voice and deep spiritual insight, TashaRenèe carries a mantle for healing the whole woman, guiding women into intimacy with Abba Father and the restoration of their spiritual identity. Her work helps women reclaim their voice, heal their inner wounds, and birth the purpose and destiny placed within them.

She is also the founder of TableForYOU, a sacred community devoted to authentic connection and sisterhood. TashaRenèe holds an Honorary Doctorate of Ministry Leadership and has devoted her life to helping women live whole, lead well, and dwell deeply in the secret place with God.

The Bitter Wait

The Sour to Sweet Surprise

| Tami Tenbarge |

*"She is clothed with strength and dignity,
and she laughs without fear of the future."*
Proverbs 31:25 NLT

Chapter 10

The bitter wait keeps echoing through my life's song like a relentless chorus I'd rather not have to keep singing. Learning to surrender to God's timing—and to exist in that uncomfortable in-between—is no small task for a woman like me: impatient, driven, ambitious to a fault. I have to remind myself again and again that waiting time is not wasted time. Because even when everything feels still, God—the Way Maker—is moving in the unseen, aligning people, moments, and miracles with a precision only Heaven could orchestrate.

And now that it's probably obvious from my musical play on words that I love to worship, let me kick things off with a little motivational moment I once gave while leading worship … one I will never live down.

We were mid-set, and I was feeling extra energized—full of passion, full of fire, full of "let's go after God with everything we've got." So I grabbed the mic and said something along the lines of, "Sing it with us and raise those hands—let's go balls to the wall worshiping Jesus tonight!"

Why I chose that phrase—one I had never used a day in my life—I truly don't know. It escaped before I even knew it was forming, far too fast for me to catch and return to sender. But judging by the wide eyes, dropped jaws, and the eruption of laughter, I learned very quickly that there are, in fact, far better word choices to motivate people without completely derailing the flow of worship.

Thankfully, it was an auditorium full of teenagers … but still. Not my finest moment. And trust me, the ones who witnessed it have made sure I never forget it. My naivete became their favorite running joke.

I'm pretty sure I accidentally made Jesus laugh that night. Which isn't such a bad thing I suppose, considering the heart of our Heavenly Father is joy. If the joy of the Lord is our strength like it says in Nehemiah 8:10, that means God intentionally tied joy to strength.

Why?

Because He knew we would need strength, and He knew the source would be joy.

Not striving. Not performance. Not pressure.

Joy.

His joy over us. Our joy in Him.

What a blessing we don't have to choose between the two; His design is a package deal. They always come together—in abundance.

Strength that flows from knowing we are loved. Strength that isn't manufactured or earned—it's simply received.

Proverbs 31:25 declares that she is clothed with strength and dignity, and she laughs without fear of the future. Though the verse doesn't point to one woman, my mind races straight to Sarah—Abraham's wife, the woman who heard an impossible promise spoken into a body long past its prime. "And I will bless her and give you a son from her! Yes, I will bless her richly, and she will become the mother of many nations. Kings of nations will be among her descendants" (Genesis 17:16, NLT). At 90 years old, she did the most human thing imaginable: She laughed. This wasn't out of disbelief alone, but at the sheer absurdity of hope arriving so late it defied biology itself. How could she not laugh? The very idea of cradling a newborn at that age felt like an inconceivable joke wrapped in holy mystery.

And yet, I understand her more than I ever expected. By 37, I had nearly convinced myself that I misheard God, and that I needed to let go of the hope for a son. After five relentless years of loss—five seasons where hope rose only to be shattered again—my heart learned to brace itself. My prayers fell silent and my spirit quietly surrendered to the belief that the door had closed for good.

But God has never bowed to human timelines or a biological clock. We learn this in Genesis 21 when He blesses Sarah (age 90) and Abraham (age 100) with Isaac, which means "laughter." a reminder of her initial disbelief. But when God has a plan, He doesn't need our belief. When He moves, He does so with a force that shatters doubt, dismantles disappointment, and silences every whispered lie from the enemy.

Because when it is God's plan, nothing—not age, not grief, not the slow erosion of hope—can stand against the power of His hand.

The woman described in Proverbs 31 is the kind of woman I am learning to become—steadfast, steady, and anchored in a strength that doesn't originate from her own resolve, but from knowing the Father's heart. The more I understand who He is, the deeper

A freedom that lets me release a soft snicker in the face of adversity, not out of denial, but out of confidence—because my God has a reputation for transforming the most bitter lemons life can hurl into the sweetest testimony a soul could ever taste.

my trust sinks its roots. Not only do I rely on Him to walk with me through hardship, but I lean on His wisdom to steady my steps, guide my responses, and lift me above what tries to pull me under.

And there is a quiet kind of freedom in that. A freedom that lets me release a soft snicker in the face of adversity, not out of denial, but out of confidence—because my God has a reputation for transforming the most bitter lemons life can hurl into the sweetest testimony a soul could ever taste.

"Taste and see that the Lord is good."
(Psalm 34:8, NIV)

Lemons to Lemonade Story

After enduring five consecutive pregnancy losses in 5 years, it was my 37th birthday, and my friend, Mistie, wrote on my Facebook timeline:

> "Happy birthday to my dear friend, Tami. It's safe to say Tami has been served quite a few lemons in her life. The thing I love the most about her is she doesn't just make lemonade. She opens a lemonade stand with 7 employees and plans for expansion. She inspires me to dream big and challenges me to cultivate and pursue those dreams. I am honored to call her friend."

That's my Mistie, always adding a dose of inspiration and humor to all that she does.

But the reality is that year, I hadn't laughed much. The devastation of a second surgery to remove an ectopic pregnancy had left me wounded in more ways than one. Add to that a blighted ovum the year before, another tubal pregnancy the year prior, and two miscarriages—five losses in 5 years. Plus, the infertility specialist delivered the kind of news that knocks the wind out of you: less than a 10% chance of conceiving. I was down to one fragile tube, layers of scar tissue, only a handful of eggs left—and the ones I did have were, in his words, "old." I had officially entered the category of a geriatric pregnancy patient. With nothing working in our favor, the buildup of pain, confusion, and hollowed-out hope felt unbearable. If I'm being honest, it stirred a raw resentment in me—a quiet wrestling I didn't have words for. Joy felt lost, faith had thinned, and laughter seemed like a thing of the past.

Hadn't I endured enough already? After everything else I had walked through years before, I truly believed I had "paid my dues" in suffering. So, when another season of crushing disappointment swept in, it felt cruel—almost personal. I was a good woman. I worked hard. I loved Jesus. I served faithfully in my church. I had been fortunate to find my soulmate in Chris when I remarried, and though we were blessed with a baby girl three years into our marriage, we desperately wanted to complete our family with a son. We adored our two daughters, but God had given me vivid dreams of three children—two girls and a boy. I trusted those dreams were from Him, so much that I bought three of everything for the kids— three matching Easter baskets, three matching Christmas stockings, even three matching little pumpkin patch yard signs with the girls' names inscribed on two and the third one left blank for the day our baby boy would arrive. So to be told "no" by God at every attempt to have that third child—it went against everything I knew and trusted about my Heavenly Father.

After my pity party ran its course, I finally asked God, "If not this … then what?"

But if I'm honest, it came out more like an adult-sized tantrum:

"OK God! I get it! You don't think I'm a good enough mom to have any more babies—SO IF NOT THIS, THEN WHAT DO YOU WANT FROM ME!"

And in that moment, He spoke—gently, almost like a parable whispered into my spirit.

He reminded me of the Christmas gift I once bought for my daughter, the one she begged for. I had hidden it months in advance on the top shelf of the closet, waiting for the perfect moment to give it to her. As the day approached, her persistence nearly broke me—I wanted to give in early—but I couldn't. I knew the gift would mean more in its appointed time.

"That's how it feels for Me right now," He said. "As your Father, I'm holding something precious for you. Trust My timing. I will be faithful to bless you with all three children I promised. But first … I want to birth something else in you."

Excuse me, did you say birth something else?

That stopped me in my tracks because I didn't know you could birth anything but a baby.

"Alright, God," I replied. "You have my full attention now."
And that's when it began.

Over the weeks and months that followed, God started to birth a vision inside me—a movement for women, rooted in faith, designed to equip and mobilize His daughters into leadership for kingdom impact. That vision became **Free To Be Women's Leadership**.

Because when a woman discovers who she is in Christ, when she uncovers the purpose she was placed on this earth to fulfill, and is trained to lead with confidence and *authentegrity*, everything changes. Her relationships shift. Her work deepens. Her future ignites with a new kind of vision and passion. She is finally free to become *all* that God intended for her to *be*.

> *"Where there is no vision, the people perish."*
> *(Proverbs 29:18, KJV)*

The vision that Proverbs 29:18 speaks of is what keeps a person alive on the inside long before they die on the outside.

Don't let yourself become the woman who loses sight of her God-given purpose once raising littles ends or her career plateaus—only to stop truly living long before her life is over. Refuse to let that be your story!

As Free to Be took shape—growing from a personal ministry into an official nonprofit—the vision was simple but powerful: to equip women with leadership development training merged with the power of the Holy Spirit. We wanted to create an intersection where women and students could be educated, equipped, and empowered to carry God's presence into every arena they enter—boardrooms, business meetings, school campuses, sports teams, small groups, you name it—so they could lead with a holy boldness that impacts others for Christ.

Free to Be exists to help women step into their God-given purpose, not remain shackled by regret. So not surprisingly, many of the women God brought across my path felt ruined by the devastation of divorce, addiction, miscarriage, or past failures. They carried the same hopelessness I once did. But God redeemed my life after my ex's affair. One day, He whispered to me—the broken, divorced, single mama I was—and said He had purposed me for something new in the season ahead. That was the moment I knew it was time to stop living in the past and prepare for the new thing God was calling me to do.

What began as a small gathering of women has now grown into a movement designed to equip and mobilize women into leadership across the nations. Free To Be conference event halls are filled with hundreds of women every year ready to grow in their purposes and develop their gifts. Thousands have attended our annual "Free to Worship" outdoor community worship nights. Our Free To Be international retreats have become a sacred space for women to experience breakthroughs and life changes in ways only our Creator can facilitate. My favorite part is watching God birth new callings, businesses, nonprofits, books, podcasts, 5Ks, and ministries inside women who once believed their story had stopped being written.

And to think it all began with my frustrated question: **If not this, then what?**

You see, the rubble of what once was often becomes the platform God stands you on to elevate you into what you were always meant to be. We think when our world temporarily gets turned upside down that it's game over; but "Jesus Laughs" because He sees the entire picture, and He knows the game is just getting started!

One day, as I looked into my son's beautiful blue eyes, God reminded me: I would have never launched Free To Be if He had given me what I wanted in my timing. But because I pressed into Him—through anger, disappointment, and surrender—and because I obeyed when He told me what to create, He honored His promise. The very next month after that first Free To Be conference, I conceived a viable pregnancy. Six Free To Be conferences later, I laugh at the irony. We don't get to tell God our plan and expect Him to hop on it. Our job is to surrender to His will, trust His timing, and move when He says, "It's go-time, sister!"

And the joke was on me in another way, too. Who was I to lead a women's leadership movement when I had never been surrounded by a large network of women? In fact, my story felt like the opposite. Call it "girls being girls" or "girl drama," but throughout adolescence and into adulthood, I—like many women—struggled to find trustworthy friendships that built up rather than tore down.

But that's exactly how God works. He exposes a need, then calls you to fill it. If I wanted women to know the life-giving power of authentic, Christ-centered female friendships, then I had to model it—and cultivate a community where they could experience it. That's why Free To Be grew so quickly. High-capacity women don't want surface level friendships. We want meaningful, rich connections to other like-minded women who desire to talk about things that matter and intercede for one another. It's one thing to see women dressed up, laughing over dinner. It's another to watch those same women sitting on my couch afterward, baring their souls about a struggle—a broken marriage, a wayward child, an addiction that started as a coping mechanism—before an all-out laying on of hands prayer meeting erupts, where we're bombarding Heaven together!

So why did God call me to serve women and equip them to become the leaders they were meant to be? And why did God prompt you to pick up this book and read knowing all you've been through? Because He wastes nothing. He takes what the enemy meant for evil and turns it for good. Because redemption matters. Because when wrongs get righted His way, vengeance is the Lord's, and that feels good. Because people are desperate for the kind of hope that says, *No matter what caused my brokenness, there is a God who will make all things beautiful in His time.*

Free To Be began as coffee dates and Chick-fil-A lunches with women who, like me, felt paralyzed by a divorce I never saw coming. But they watched me get back up—hand in hand with Jesus—and come out stronger on the other side. I know that if an abundant life is possible for me, it's more than possible for everyone who says, *God, I surrender to your will and to your way.* So anytime I could encourage another woman facing betrayal or rejection, I went. And on my way, I asked God to fill my mouth and shine through the dark crevasses of my pain so they could see the light of hope in their own … and become free to be everything He purposed them to be. Jesus doesn't just fix things—He sweetens them. And He promises we will laugh again, but this time without fear of the future.

The *Lemonade*

| He doesn't just fix things. He sweetens them. |

What have you been asking God for in your waiting season?

Could there possibly be something different God is trying to birth in you during this in-between period? If so, what comes up for you when you ask God the question, **"If not this, then what?"**

"She is clothed with strength and dignity, and she laughs without fear of the future."
Proverbs 31:25 NLT

| Meet Tami Tenbarge |

Tami Tenbarge is a John Maxwell certified Leadership Speaker, Trainer, & Coach serving thousands in the corporate and religious sectors each year. As the founder and visionary of Free to Be Women's Leadership, a nonprofit dedicated to equipping and mobilizing women into leadership across the nations, she has a heart to help women find their identity in Christ and live out their God-given purpose.

With more than twenty-five years experience in both ministry and the corporate leadership space, she has inspired thousands of women to step boldly into their God-given purpose through conferences, international retreats, student leadership events, and worship gatherings. Tami is passionate about helping women connect the dots between their pain, passion, and purpose so they can lead with intention and live fully alive in Christ!

As a speaker and author of 30 Days to an Unstoppable You, she encourages women to reject average and embrace the abundant life God created them to live. Connect with her to learn more at freetobe.online

Sweet Jesus

The Sustenance from the Sour

| Tamra Andress |

*"Taste and see that the Lord is good; blessed
is the one who takes refuge in him."
Psalm 34:8 NIV*

Chapter 11

To begin, you have to know how I know Jesus laughs.

Confession: I have a tendency to judge you. To hold a bit of a grudge. And perhaps determine your worth and value solely on one small, seemingly insignificant choice. To me, this feels grandiose. This is vital. This is life or death. So in brotherly/sisterly love, I'll tell you outright. That way, you're prepared and there is no confusion if I don't dwell in your space for too long. Here it is … your taste in toilet paper matters (to me). That's right. Is it 2-ply? Does it scratch me as I gingerly clean a sacred area of my holy vessel? And slightly less important, but still noted, is it pulled over the top or are you a bottom dweller?

You know how I know Jesus gets the final laugh, even on my silly misplaced valuation of a home, a person, a restaurant, or a place of business? Because, I swear, every single time I have to replace the empty roll. Whether before, during, or after the duty. And this is what rings in my heart as I chuckle with the Lord, in spite of its rich bountiful softness or its crude weightless rigidity: "I came to serve, not to be served."

"For even the Son of Man did not come
to be served, but to serve."
(Mark 10:45, NIV)

So begrudgingly, yet kindly, I prepare the new roll time and time again. And as I daily die to my fleshly needs and take up my cross daily (Luke 9:23), Jesus' vote of humor and correction guides me into acceptance, patience, perspective, and love—and of course, a little chuckle.

If this can happen over a roll of toilet paper, how much more does the Father prepare one-liners for us that will wreck and remake our character and our souls each day, each season, and throughout our lifetime? He'll humble us in holy humor.

This is the beauty of an intimate relationship. One that knows you so well, that they would go out of their way to talk to you in the most vulnerable of places … even the stinkiest. A bathroom. I chuckle as I'm reminded of Psalm 139:7 (NIV), where David wrote, "Where can I go from your Spirit?" For heaven's sake. Really, Jesus? I stand corrected and humbled as I share this true, yet not so proud, part of my persona with you, and I hope I can create some correlation before I dive into other moments where Jesus has laughed at me, with me, and even in spite of me. This isn't to help you understand me any more than you do at this point, but it's about sharing the joyous Jesus I have come to know and love as friend.

You know—the kind of friend that you can stay up laughing with for hours into the dark of the night not even fully sure what's so funny. Or for me—since I'm an early bird—the wee hours of the morning over coffee. Friends who will wear their morning eye and pimple patches with you while you sip your lattes and eat the morning Word as if it were a decadent donut, only to look up and realize that the eye patches are now at the bottom of your cheeks and completely useless to their purpose. Those friends. We try to be fancy on the veranda, but our old, holey (not holy) PJs and concerted efforts to be regal land far from the target. And yet, we laugh until we pee our pants, simply because it's more fun to be of good cheer than to take ourselves too seriously. But sometimes the sour seems to outlast the sweet, and joy feels as far away as the toilet paper holder that's oddly on the other side of the room. Whose arms are actually that long? Lord. Help me. And please, give me more delightful veranda moments to laugh with you instead of wince and cry.

Discovering Decadent Delights

A decade had passed. I had become a whole new person. My identity was secured, instead of wavering with the wind. My decisions were rooted and contemplative, instead of shallow and always selfish. I guess some would call this wisdom. The kind that can only come with years of trial and error and triumph after many failures. But I would call it sweet joy after tart, tasteless seasons of unbearable sour suffering; because if you suffer well, it will lead to sweet sustenance in Him. This is the journey after all, right?

> "Not only so, but we also glory in our sufferings, because we know that suffering produces perseverance; perseverance, character; and character, hope. And hope does not put us to shame, because God's love has been poured out into our hearts through the Holy Spirit, who has been given to us." (Romans 5:3–5, NIV)

Like Job, the view from my windows hadn't shifted too much in this 10-year span, though the fine lines had set into my face from both stress and deep satisfaction. While my family had grown in stature spiritually and physically, a Facebook image on my screen—not so surprisingly—hit a faulty nerve. A flash from the past. A healthy dose of humble pie. A grim vantage point of loss and lack. I was but a shell of who I am today, and yet now, more than ever, as I've pursued knowing Jesus' purpose, plan, and pathway to an abundant life, I can be grateful for that version of me. That version that clung to the flicker of sweet hope that I had tasted and seen in minute sipping sessions with God in my adolescence. The moments at a friend's church weekend retreat during my middle school years. Scripture reading times with a friend's dad at their kitchen counter. Microphone and stage moments at youth groups as I worshipped and shared about a "friend," who I really faintly knew. Small groups with people that later became mentors and shining examples of His steadfast presence in my life. Even echoes of worship songs and words that were hidden in my heart for years were instantly recalled when I came to surrender my life to Jesus once and for all.

You see, like Hansel and Gretel, Jesus leaves crumbs. He is the bread of life after all (John 6:35, NIV). (Bada bing, bada boom … see what I did there!?) He doesn't leave or forsake you. And there will always be a palpable sweetness even in the sourest of seasons. I process Job's journey in conjunction with mine. Where Jesus laughed in the face of the enemy once He got the final say over Job's life.

"The Lord said to Satan, 'Very well, then,
everything he has is in your power, but on the
man himself do not lay a finger.' Then Satan
went out from the presence of the Lord."
(Job 1:12, NIV)

"The Lord said to Satan, 'Very well, then,
he is in your hands; but you must spare his life.'"
(Job 2:6, NIV)

The same conversation may have happened about me. "You can take it all away from her. Her businesses. Her health. Her 'happiness.' Her family. Her security. All she knows. Her talents and treasures. But you may not take her life." This has been my story. In one decade, the enemy has come hard after everything that I'd call "sweet" only to help me, to propel me, to even drag me to the feet of Jesus to discover how sweet sustenance actually only exists by and through Him. The enemy came to prove God wrong, but God will get the last laugh, just like Job's redemption story. I stand on that promise.

> *"The Lord blessed the latter part*
> *of Job's life more than the former part."*
> *(Job 42:12, NIV)*

In one decade, the enemy has come hard after everything that I'd call "sweet" only to help me, to propel me, to even drag me to the feet of Jesus to discover how sweet sustenance actually only exists by and through Him.

It's worthwhile we journey, like Job, through Satan's faulty attempts in various areas of my life, so that you too can gain perspective on just how laughable the enemy's lack of creativity and absurdities actually are once you've surpassed their sour stings.

"Her businesses" — Upon releasing my life to the Lord, He asked me to step into my identity as a daughter. Not as a go-getter business woman and entrepreneur. But as a wife, mother, and restful child. I let go of two businesses that I had worked my entire 20s to build. In truth, it felt more like a forced quit than a free-will choice. The enemy had seeped into my place of work through screens and the allure of a life and a facade of love that wasn't my reality—just as he did when dial-up internet entered my home as a child. Again, not creative. The enemy knew my weak points and fleshly imagination would lead me down the same path of internal and relational destruction. (You can read more about that season of life in my first book, "Always Becoming: sex, shame & Love.") So beyond a reputation and identity destruction, he also attacked my sense of security in finances as one of the businesses—that served three global markets—had quite the hefty dollar sign connected to it. But in one Jesus encounter in my living room, one taste of His fulfillment, the force didn't come from my husband or another external source, but from His sweetness. As I released those roles, what felt unsettling and sour, in His succulent kindness, brought me a deep sigh of relief. I discovered my recklessness was rooted in a performance-driven exhaustive race toward the world's version of success—one that would lead not just to a sour, but a rotten, life of lemons.

So where does Jesus' punch line come in? The first call. The first time I heard Him summon me into my "new work," Kingdom work. I sat in the pews of our new spirit-filled church home when a guest speaker came in to share about a worship school called Burn 24-7. I felt like the speaker was speaking in a cyclone specifically to me. No one else was in the room. He had tunnel vision into my soul as his words penetrated my spirit. He shared the mission, and I heard the call. "You are going to do this." And so I did. What's hysterical was that, on day one of the yearlong experience, the students all did introductions. I was used to having a book-long resume with accolades that "fit or impressed," and this time I had nothing to showcase besides my obedient, unsure "yes" to the Lord. The room was filled with seasoned musicians and worship vocalists. I was the only one who loved to sing (but was only on the mic at youth group) and never played an instrument besides a momentary strum or "Chopsticks" piano tune. Jesus chuckled. As I sat feeling insignificant and unworthy, session by session, He poured sugar on my soul, guiding me into a new understanding and expression of worship that cemented Him as King and me as His daughter and dancer. Worship comes in so many expressions. In all that He redeemed, He even took the sour of what dance had become in my 20s and reestablished my body and its purpose by honoring Him through my passion for movement and flow. A few short years later, He set me on a new path—one without striving—to establish a new business. F.I.T. in Faith Press was established with the mission of gathering His children, pulling out the gold in them, and helping them establish their stories in the marketplace—transforming their messages into movements and global ministries. Sweet redemption. All was not lost, it was recycled for His glory. This same business is how you are currently holding this book in your hands. F.I.T. in Faith Press is not for me, by me, or to bolster anything I have done or can do, but to publish His glorious deeds in all He continues to do each and every day. I pray that, whatever state of pursuit you are in towards "success," you first secure your identity in Him. That you identify your business always as Kingdom business. And your lifelong pursuit isn't consumed by fleshly desire, but secured by a deep calling towards your ultimate purpose of glorifying Him and making heaven crowded.

"Her health" — I've always known fitness and nutrition as common practices and responsible tools for discipline. Because of that, I've always felt entitled to a

> *All was not lost, it was recycled for His glory.*

positive, healthy outcome. If A, then B. Practically speaking, it should equate. But as you know, just as when sin entered the garden, the enemy's twists and thwarts have seeped into our environment, our food, our land, our pharmaceuticals—and sadly, our sugar. (*This is why His sweetness is the only true satisfaction.*) Throughout the years, there have been many aspects of my health that I've had to focus on. Sixteen years of gymnastics led me to endless chiropractic care and a back brace in middle school. I never considered what that would look like long term, but due to scoliosis, pregnancy had my body in shambles with sciatica and varicose veins. My vision also started deteriorating mildly—but still noticeably—in college, which required attention. Could I have blamed the enemy here? Perhaps. But let's not get on a soapbox with the "not all things are demonic" conversation, as I'm very aware that in the testing of our faith, God may be the one serving up the lemons from time to time—but lemons aren't the lesson; the laughter on the other side is the proof.

Even still, on this side of heaven, full healing may not bring the fullness of freedom in our bodies that we crave. But I surely wanted to experience relief. After my encounter with Christ, I went on a health journey. I was able to get LASIK eye surgery, and though I almost could have gone blind due to a nurse's wrong prescription write-up, I didn't. But now, God and I chuckle. Every time I look at light-day or night—there is an ambient rainbow in my peripheral vision that has never faded even a decade later. He is my source of sight. He gave me eyes to see. And if this was the only gift He gave me to remind me of Himself daily, it would be enough. Especially if you know my passion for the vibrancy and promise fulfillment of rainbows.

> "And God said, 'This is the sign of the covenant I am making between me and you and every living creature with you, a covenant for all generations to come: I have set my rainbow in the clouds, and it will be the sign of the covenant between me and the earth.'" (Genesis 9:12–13, NIV)

But this was only one of the millions of miracles I've experienced. His sweetness doesn't run out for His children. Abundance is His name.

Soon after my LASIK eye surgery, I pursued a treatment to ease the pain of my varicose veins. Little did I know that the Lord had more healing in store for me. That day, He told me, "I'm renewing your bloodline," and I had a revelation of His divine blood running through my veins. This marked the beginning of my journey with generational curse breaking that took years and years of battling. Years later, in a supernatural *Sozo* session (*Sozo* is a Greek word used over 100 times in the New Testament meaning to save, heal, deliver, and make whole), my pastor and I both witnessed the same thing: an onion-like lotus flower blooming at the center of a cord being disconnected from a dead source and reconnected to Jesus like a sort of umbilical cord. It felt like the finale of the unhealthy ties the enemy had established for generations in both my husband's and my family lines. You see, we often expect God to heal us in the natural, but His work will always remain in the supernatural, even if evidence in the flesh is secured and recognized, too.

I would have been satisfied in this category of health, but as you age, more things surface. I received a diagnosis of Hashimoto's a couple years ago through a blood panel. I felt like my body had rejected me. I was even frustrated with God. If I lined myself up against others, I was the healthy one. The disciplined one. The one that fasted daily for nearly 7 years. How could this be true? Instead of partnering with this new label, I chose the natural and prayerful path to healing. He is my sustainer after all. I didn't take medication—not because I'm anti-medicine, but because I believed there was a more effective way for me to pursue restoration. I'm still walking this one out, especially in this new era and adventure with my body, but I have hope. In fact, my hope has grown. A year after my diagnosis, I experienced a miraculous healing in my back.

What felt impossible, after decades of wishful thinking that then shifted to prayerful anticipation, finally came true. My back became physically aligned to match my spiritual stature during a healing service at my church. I stood at the back of the room, holding my dear friend's baby girl. We were praying for ourselves and/or others who needed a physical touch from the Great Physician. Like many times before, I focused on my spine. But quickly my thoughts and heart shifted towards this angelic baby girl. I looked at her beautiful face, that was being affected by eczema flare-ups, and I prayed, "Lord, pass by me. I don't need this healing, but give it to this baby, give it to my babies, give it to the children." It was a fairly fleeting thought, to be honest, but still a desperation of my heart in that brief moment of focus. And in that moment, I felt my spine realign. My hips shifted in the standing position I had stood for years. The pastor asked anyone to raise their hand if they had felt a shift, a burning sensation, or any response from Heaven. Even 9 years into my miraculous encounters with God, I still stood in mild disbelief. *No, I just made that up. Why would He do that now, after all these years? What did I do to deserve this?* I went weeks without telling anyone. In those same weeks, I had zero back pain. I slept soundly. I went nearly 5 months without chiropractic care—the longest stretch in my life over the past 20 years. I started to tell people. I told my husband. I shared it with the mama of that baby girl I was holding. I even relished what happened to Forrest Frank in his miraculous spinal adjustment that led to the viral song connected to this very situation, "God's Got My Back." And then, after a surf session, I felt my back tweak a bit and instantly thought, "I knew it wasn't healed." As I divulged the news to a friend on the shoreline, I bared my soul to her in tears as the sun hit my cheeks. I shared my unbelief and the many prayers I prayed—much like the father who wrestled with doubt while praying for his son's healing.

"I do believe; help me overcome my unbelief!"
(Mark 9:24, NIV)

I felt unworthy of His healing when I knew so many others were in dire need. But God's sweetness is enough; it's plentiful, it's intentional, and it's ours for the savoring. That moment on the beach, as we prayed, I knew this healing was an extra gift just for me in a season that had been really dark, and that the Lord had asked me to "stay and stand" for my marriage and my family. It's surely not out of His character to give us savory gifts that satisfy every part of who we are. We're meant to walk in this Edenic expression of companionship with God. Laughing in the garden, because it's our birthright. Free from the bondage of even our bodies' insufficiencies and weaknesses. I've gone to the chiropractor intermittently (but not regularly) since this time, and I've used Icy Hot for back relief. I've had some restless nights, too, from back pain. But I'm still standing in the belief that my spine has been repositioned to a place of stature and that Hashimoto's will not get the final say in my health, not even because of my obedience, but because of His generous, lavish love to see me healed and whole as He intended. If you're holding on to a promise of healing … don't write it off. Even in your unbelief, I pray He sweetens your knowledge of who He is and satisfies your unspoken cravings.

It's worth noting that even though I took care of myself in the natural, I could not have anticipated the way the Lord wanted to heal me supernaturally. I thought I was tending to a vision problem, and I ended up with rainbow reminders of His goodness. I thought I was relieving vein pain, only to get a new blood infusion of His divine DNA. I thought I was getting healed from a lifelong scoliosis prognosis, but instead was given stature and alignment for the heavy lifting in my marital story.

I can keep going, for the sour and sweet dance with the Lord doesn't end—at least, I don't anticipate it will. The longer I've been sipping lemonade with Jesus, the more I revel in His laughter and His perfect plan in spite of what the enemy tries to kill, steal, and destroy.

> *"The One enthroned in heaven laughs;*
> *the Lord scoffs at them."*
> *(Psalm 2:4, NIV)*

You must know, the enemy doesn't stop at God's miracle or presence; though he flees at His name, he will keep coming after us. It's our steadfastness to stand on His promises—His "Yes and Amens" (2 Corinthians 1:20) to our lives, our identity, and our eternal reward—that keeps the enemy's tantalizing, deceptive tactics to burn our tastebuds at bay. As I mentioned earlier, the enemy came after my happiness, my family, my security, and all I knew, but with each passing sour experience, the old me that the enemy so easily taunted, started to be pre-conditioned to God's delight. (Essentially, my tastebuds were better at detecting when the enemy was slipping me a roofie.) His delight is so sweet, in fact, just as all Job had lost was multiplied, I write this today with a new sweet seed in my belly—after nearly 12 years of waiting for a child. I wouldn't be here if He didn't carry me through to see it come to fruition. This blessing of a third child is going to taste even sweeter having gone through the muddling trials of life—and of course perfectly timed for a sweet summer of sipping lemonade in the sunshine. Talk about bearing fruit.

"Taste and see that the Lord is good" (Psalm 34:8, NIV)—and then believe it! Over and over again. For as long as you live.

The *Lemonade*

| I tasted the sour, trusted His sweetness,
and learned—God's humor is holy. |

Where in your life have you been bracing for bitterness instead of expecting God's goodness—and what would it look like to intentionally "taste and see" His presence there, even if the outcome feels uncertain?

What beliefs, phrases, or past experiences have shaped how you expect life to taste—and how might God be inviting you to take refuge in Him rather than in self-protection, numbing, or resignation?

"Taste and see that the Lord is good;
blessed is the one who takes refuge in him."
Psalm 34:8 NIV

| Meet Tamra Andress |

Tamra Andress is a TEDx and keynote speaker, 8x best-selling author, and founder of F.I.T. in Faith Press, a Christian publishing house dedicated to equipping authors to release Heaven's messages into the world. Through her publishing work, Tamra helps faith-driven leaders transform their testimonies into impactful books that inspire transformation and Kingdom influence.

She also hosted seven seasons of "The Messenger Movement" Podcast, a top-ranking show equipping faith-first leaders to amplify their voices and steward the power of their stories.

As founder and president of The Founder Collective, Tamra leads a growing community of faith-driven entrepreneurs through discipleship, leadership development, and the annual FounderCon experience held the first week of November, where leaders gather to be equipped, connected, and activated for greater Kingdom impact.

Above all, Tamra is a devoted wife to a fellow entrepreneur, mama to two spirited kid-preneurs, and known as a Kingdom connector who helps believers boldly share their God-given messages with the world.

Acknowledgments

To His laughing daughters, the authors of this work. Those who bravely step into His adoring delight each day, no matter the heartache or hardship. Like your Father in Heaven, you *"laugh at the days to come"* (Proverbs 31:25b). Your steadfast resilience inspires, equips, and sends forth other Kingdom children so they, too, can thrive and stand in the saturated sweetness of His love, joy, and peace.

To our incredible detail-oriented editor, Anne. Your partnership in this project—carefully combing through every word while sending uplifting messages of encouragement—has strengthened His Church in ways that will expand far beyond what you can see. Your faithful work will reach into the hearts of every reader and deepen their personal journey with Jesus.

To our talented designer, Becky. You bring vibrant life to the mission of F.I.T. in Faith Press, adding beauty and excellence to every layer of our books and their messages. We deeply value your gifts and creativity and treasure the way they serve the hearts and souls of those who will encounter these pages.

And lastly, to our final hour addition, talented sketch artist, Kylie Bromwell. You brought His laughter to life with your beautiful gift.

Thank each of you tremendously.

A Boutique Publishing & Media House for Founders, Innovators & Trailblazers!

F.I.T. Founders, Innovators & Trailblazers — exists to cultivate and deploy Kingdom messengers called to build movements, not simply publish books.

From manuscript to microphone to movement, we design aligned pathways that transform revelation into measurable KINGDOM impact!

GET STARTED ON YOUR PUBLISHING JOURNEY TODAY!

PROFIT INDENITY

Reveal Your Passion and Spiritual Gifts
Connection to Start & Grow Your Business

TAKE THE QUIZ TODAY!

HAVE YOU EVER WONDERED?

What your purpose is?

How you could use your giftings as a global messenger for God?

How your spiritual gifts are connected to your calling?

How your passion propels your profit?

Ladies! Beauty Awaits from the inside-out and outside-in.

We will explore every detail of God's wondrous creation. Starting with YOU! This wellness retreat is an immersive experience intended to get you back to the basics (mind, body, and HOLY spirit) by heightening your senses to what matters most: your vertical alignment, so you can horizontally serve, share, and SHINE!

Fella's! The Great Outdoor Awaits! Embark. Elevate. Expand. Explore.

Getting primal to perform at our highest potential as men, husbands, fathers, and leaders by activating our sonship. Join us on this "unforgettable, epic, and life-changing" adventure that will catalyze you to exist in your power, authority, and passion.

Contact: hello@thefoundercollective.org

Join a Messenger Movement of Founders and
Leaders who know they are ministers first, sent
into business to influence, disciple, and advance
the Kingdom from the inside out.

Together, we build businesses and movements
with purpose and lead with Kingdom authority.

COME BUILD. COME LEAD. COME BE SENT.
We are the mobilized church!

A Podcast for the Messengers!
FLOWCODE
PRIVACY.FLOWCODE.COM
SUBSCRIBE & LEAVE A REVIEW FOR A SHOUTOUT ON AIR!
MESSENGER MOVEMENT
PODCAST
Tamra Andress
The called ones.
The mobilized ones.
The ones on a mission to turn
their message into a movement!
This show was designed for Declaring Truth,
Transforming Narratives & Catalyzing Christians
to Speak, Write, Build & Testify.

Join us on a devotional journey to
Finding Joy in God AND Breaking Out of the Boxes
the World Puts Us In!
F.I.T. Press presents *More Than Enough:
The Silent Struggle of a Women's Identity*

You are more than...
More than a Religion
More Than a Mom
More than a Wife
More than My Past
More than my body
More than my job

Get the More Than Enough Devotional Companion Study Guide : A 38 page biblical resource + 9 videos www. fitinfaithmedia.com/devotional

Before she Knew JESUS

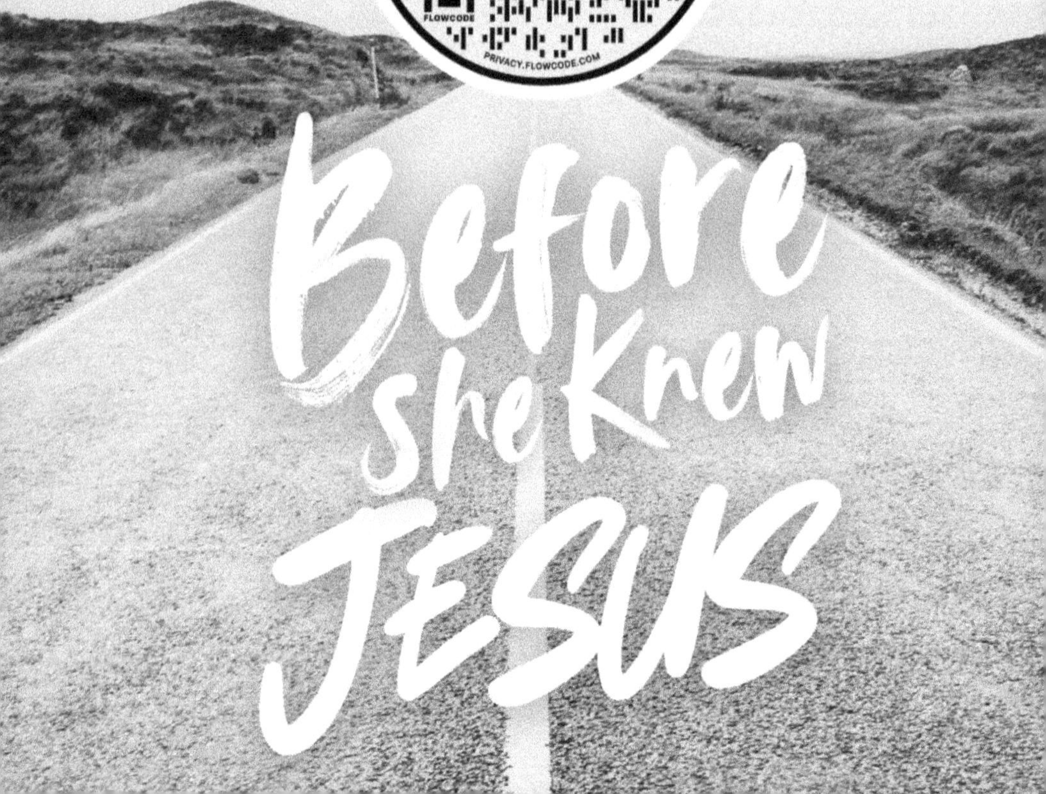

SHOP

MORE BOOKS BY

F.I.T. IN FAITH BOUTIQUE PUBLISHING HOUSE!

We are a company DEVELOPING & DEPLOYING MESSENGERS *through* publishing, podcasting and platform development!

We help develop, nurture, and grow services, retreats & events for Founders, Innovators, and Trailblazers on a mission to turn their God-given messages into movements for Kingdom expansion!